5-01

THE TAO OF SELF-DEFENSE

THE

TAO

OF

SELF-

DEFENSE

SCOTT SHAW

SAMUEL WEISER, INC.
York Beach, Maine

First published in 2000 by
SAMUEL WEISER, INC.
P.O. Box 612
York Beach, ME 03910-0612
www.weiserbooks.com

Library of Congress Cataloging-in-Publication Data

Shaw, Scott.
   The tao of self-defense / Scott Shaw.
      p. cm.
   Includes index.
   ISBN 1-57863-190-4 (pbk. : alk. Paper)
   1. Self-defense.   2. Martial arts.   I. Title.
GV1111.S39 2000
796.8—dc21   00–029005

VG

Photography by Hae Won Shin and Associates
Typeset in 11/18 Adobe Caslon
Cover and text design by Kathryn Sky-Peck

PRINTED IN THE UNITED STATES OF AMERICA

07 06 05 04 03 02 01 00
  8 7 6 5 4 3 2 1

*The paper used in this publication meets the minimum requirements of the American National
Standard for Information Sciences—Permanence of Paper for Printed Library Materials
Z39.48-1992 (R1997).*

Contents

4/30/01

Acknowledgments

Special thanks to my students Hae Won Shin and Vincent L. Spezze for helping to demonstrate the self-defense techniques presented in this book.

The chapter opening quotes come from the following works: pages 1, 35, 107, 161, Lao Tzu, *Tao Te Ching;* page 3, Su-ma Fu, *Methods of the Minister of War,* page 29, Shosan Suzuki, *The Writing of Shosan Suzuki;* pages 37, 53, 73, 161, Yagyu Munenori, *Heisho Kaden Sho— Book of Family Traditions on the Martial Arts;* page 43, 137, Miyamoto Musashi, *Book of Five Rings;* pages 73, 75, Chuang Tzu, *The Inner Chapters;* pages 81, 191, Sun Tzu, *The Art of War;* page 161, Wei Liao- tzu, a military strategist from the fourth century B.C.E.; page 161, *Huainanzi,* a classic Taoist text from the Zhou period; page 201, Wu Tzu, *The Seven Military Classics.*

Introduction

There are people who believe that the practice of the martial arts only proves useful when the need for self-defense arises. True martial arts are to be practiced in such a manner that they are useful at all times and benefit all things.

—MIYAMOTO MUSASHI

As our streets have become increasingly unsafe and random acts of violence have seemingly become the norm, it has become an absolute necessity that all of us, men and women alike, learn how to quickly and effectively defend ourselves against any would-be assailant. Yet we put off learning the techniques of personal self-defense because so many of us believe that "it will never happen to me." This is the biggest misconception we can hold! Time and time again it has been proven that we must be prepared, at all times, for an unexpected confrontation.

One of the biggest mistakes people make, in the realms of self-defense ideology, is that we believe that the weapon we carry—be it pepper spray, a stun gun, a knife, or even a gun—will be all we need to protect ourselves. Of course, these weapons may prevent certain attacks or fend off others—but what if the weapon is taken away in the heat of battle? Then, not only does the attacker possess the weapon, but it can be used against us. For this reason we must learn how to effectively defend ourselves with only our hands and feet. With this mastery we will never become physically or psychologically reliant on the weapon and we will be able to successfully defend ourselves at any time and at any place.

Mastery of self-defense does not mean that you must train directly under a martial arts master for innumerable years—though one-on-one training is very effective in gaining the understanding of self-defense basics. There are problems relating to studying with a teacher in a studio. When we do this, we are often only exposed to the unrealistic conditions presented in the martial arts studio, and students falsely believe they can effectively defend themselves on the street. Due to the years of sterile defensive drills, which are generally overly elaborate in technique and execution, what often happens is that these trained martial artists will come up against a savvy street fighter who quickly defeats them. This victory is based in the primary fact of street combat: *there are no rules on the street.*

With this as a basis of understanding, it must be additionally noted that self-defense mastery does not require that you be in enhanced physical condition. You don't need the physique of a weight lifter or a professional fighter—though enhanced physical appearance may, in fact, intimidate certain opponents. What successful self-defense mastery *does* require is based on one primary principle—you must encounter any attacking opponent with full force, defeating him before he has the ability to defeat you. At no time in the physical confrontation will you have time to question your purpose, for if you question your purpose, even for a second, your attacker possesses the potential to take advantage of your doubt and overcome you. To this end, you must begin your self-defense the moment a physical confrontation is imminent.

As you begin to master the elements of self-defense, you will come to understand that the competent self-defense technician never seeks out battles at any level, for this type of meaningless confrontational conduct is embraced only by insecure people who need to gain a sense of self-worth by physically defeating someone else. This is an extremely low level of human consciousness.

Through the techniques presented in this book, you will come to possess the understanding of how to successfully defend yourself from even the most fierce attackers. This ability is based on the fact that you never engage an attacker in battle. Instead, you defeat him *before he can ever begin* his attack. This is accomplished by landing the first strike when possible, or by simply allowing him to make all the confrontational moves, which you simply avoid. When he rushes in with a forward assault, you step back, when he lunges at you from the side, you move out of his path. By learning how to successfully fight without fighting, you remain free of injury and are allowed to become like the river—flowing to its destination, encountering and moving around all obstacles.

The Fundamentals of Self-Defense

A strong soldier is not violent.

A strong fighter is not angry.

—LAO TZU

If you enter into any confrontational situation possessing a violent mind, you have predetermined that your confrontation will be based on a force of wills and determined by who is physically and mentally the strongest.

If you go into battle possessing anger, your anger will be your driving force. Though anger can be a strong motivator, it is the leading cause of failure in battle, because you are not allowing yourself to think clearly and react naturally to a confrontational situation.

Free your mind of violence, let go of anger—even in the most violent situations—and you will be able to see your opponent for who he truly is. From this, you can intuitively view his strengths and weaknesses. From this, your instinctive mind will be allowed to operate unrestrained, and you will emerge victorious.

The Foundation of Self-Defense

*In military protocol, the warrior stands firm and speaks directly. When
deployed in battle, the warrior focuses on his duty and acts accordingly.*

*During battle, those wearing battle armor need not bow.
Those in war chariots need not follow the rules of protocol.
In times of war, one does not worry about seniority. One acts.*

*The common patterns of human behavior, during times of war,
are like inside and outside. The citizen and the warrior are
like left and right, night and day.*

—SU-MA FU

I t is imperative when choosing to master the science of modern
self-defense that you are able to separate yourself from the
formalities of everyday life when you are engaged in battle.
Confrontation is not kind, nor is it just. It is for this reason that you must
never consciously seek out battle—at any level. If it finds you, however,
you must enter into personal self-defense at the most appropriate level.

If you hesitate when defending yourself, even for a second, you allow
your adversary the potential to destroy you. Thus, in battle *fight*—in
life *be kind*.

SELF-DEFENSE 101

At the foundation of any method of effective self-defense is your own
ability to read a situation, decide upon the appropriate action, and

then implement successful techniques in order to keep yourself free from injury. In martial arts schools and self-defense courses, you are taught methods of how to encounter the various types of physical attack that may befall you: be they a punch, a body grab, or a weapons assault. It is far better, however, for you to never be forced into physical confrontation at all, for this is your only assured method of never becoming injured. To achieve this, the most basic level of self-defense, you must learn how to read physical and environmental situations and then take appropriate defensive action before a physical altercation ever finds you.

Perhaps the most disconcerting factor of this level of self-defense, especially for those who have been previously attacked, is that there is no one who can teach you a method that will keep you safe from all physical confrontations. This is in no small part due to the fact that each person who would accost you possesses a different look, a different body language, and an undisclosed reasoning for why that person would wish to instigate a physical encounter in the first place. Certainly, there are types who you may come upon who "look evil," who speak to you with an intimidating tone, or who act in a specific manner that signals you to move away. In these situations, the decision to walk or run away is obvious. It is the less obvious individuals who pose the biggest problem as you may not know exactly why you want to steer clear of them.

There are countless theories—and the word "theory" is used because that's exactly all that they are—about how you should behave if someone with ill intentions comes upon you. Some of these theories tell you to remain calm, in a nonaggressive mode, that you should speak passively to the person; others tell you to be assertive and attempt to back the opponent down. Still others say you should scream or run.

When you are accosted, no theory will work. This is because each attacker is completely different and motivated by his or her own set of irrational standards. As is the case with all areas of self-defense, you must confront every situation as it is presented to you, and react at your most effective possible level.

There are some standard, commonsense rules for conduct that can hopefully keep you free from confrontation. For example, lock your doors and windows, avoid dark isolated locations, don't place yourself in dangerous environments where hostility is imminent. If accosted, leave the location immediately before the altercation has the ability to escalate. If an attacker comes up to you in a public place, call for the help of others, and so on. All of these rules can only be applied, however, prior to a physical confrontation actually taking place or when you are located in an environment where other people are present. The sad fact is that most attackers will not come upon you in public situations. They will wait until you are alone. In these situations, your absolute, full-focused, self-defense is necessary. You cannot think or be concerned about the injurious effect you are having upon your attacker, as he or she is certainly not concerned with your well-being or you would not have been accosted in the first place. For this reason, you must master, and be willing to utilize, to the best of your ability, the most effective self-defense methods available.

FEAR

Fear is one of the most detrimental emotions you can possess not only in making yourself an effective self-defense technician, but in terms of the quality of your overall life as well. People carry fear with them. They wear it like a badge. All who encounter them know they are afraid. Thus, they attract those who would take advantage of weaker individuals.

Fear is one of the most common deterrents to conscious self-defense, for if you are scared you can't function with precise mental reasoning. As such, you will make erratic decisions—attempting to escape from your fear as opposed to encountering your current reality in the most efficient manner possible.

Fear is based in the unknown: a different race, an uncharted geographical location, or a situation you have not previously encountered. Fear is propagated by society, your family, and your friends, who have all warned you to be afraid of a specific group of people or particular locations. By possessing this mentality you never allow yourself to understand that each individual is his or her own person, each sector of a city has its own beauty and attributes.

Fear can be consciously overcome by realizing that what you are scared of is not the reality that you are currently living. Fear is something off in the distance—something that has not and may never actually occur. By encountering your fears with this formula, you will no longer be dominated by this emotion. You can encounter new people and witness them for who they truly are, and view an undiscovered environment and observe its intrinsic beauty and uniqueness.

If you are forced into a physical confrontation you must consciously let go of fear, for fear in battle does you absolutely no good. In fact, in battle, show no fear. An assailant who sees that you are not afraid may choose to leave the altercation altogether as the assailant will understand that you will not be easily overpowered.

To forego fear, encounter all human beings, new environments, and unfamiliar situations with wonder and respect. Never bring to them unfounded and predetermined suppositions. From this, you will possess no fear and you will be able to live your life with a new level of perfection.

VICTIM MENTALITY

Being a victim is a state of mind. It is what you do with the experience of loss, which in turn determines whether or not you become a lifelong victim. A victim is an individual who has lost an altercation and, because of this the person is dominated by that experience for the rest of his or her life. Everywhere this person goes, he or she is scared—expecting a similar negative experience to occur. The victim mentally brings the same situations into the life experience—over and over.

The person who is not a victim may have lost battles in the past, but realizes that life is a step-by-step process. Though he or she may not have liked the experience of losing, this individual has learned what could be learned from it. The non-victim has become stronger, and has moved on with life, becoming a better and more whole individual.

WINNING AND LOSING

You cannot win all altercations. Winning or losing is all a state of mind. If you learn from your seeming loss, your are, in fact, a winner—as you have become a stronger, more complete individual. From the opposite perspective, if we have won many confrontations and are constantly seeking to prove ourselves in battle, there will eventually be somebody who will beat us. Thus, the conscious self-defense technician never seeks out battle. If battle is forced upon us, we proceed in the most conscious and effective manner possible. Then we leave the experience behind us, not attempting to gain ego gratification from this seeming victory.

REMAINING CONSCIOUS IN BATTLE

The question often arises, "How do we remain conscious in the all-engulfing randomness of battle?" There are two primary methods to achieve this. One is partner practice. The second is mental visualization.

From partner practice we learn, through personal experience, the most efficient method to deal with each style of physical attack. Thus, if we are accosted, we have already worked through the scenario and know how to most effectively deal with it.

Through the practice of mental visualization in relation to self-defense, we detail in our minds the most effective method to encounter each type of assault. By running the battle scenarios on a mental level, we train ourselves in self-defense by using mental imagery.

By learning these two practices, we have just upped the potential for becoming more secure as we move around our neighborhood and our world. We can consciously refine how to defend ourselves in all environments, and from each of the various types of attack. Once we possess this sense of mental security, we also *project* that mind-set to the world. Therefore, when we encounter people, they experience the inner power we possess. Thus, they will not thoughtlessly challenge us to battle, as they intuitively know we cannot be easily defeated.

Learn, practice, and master the techniques of self-defense. Then, project that inner self-confidence to the world. This is the best first line of defense!

ENVIRONMENTAL SELF-DEFENSE

The unfortunate reality about life is that we can be accosted by an attacker in virtually any location, at any time. Each physical location is unique and possesses its own environmental constraints. For this reason, there is no singular method of physical self-defense that will universally protect us in all geographical locations.

To master environmental self-defense, we must not only understand how to effectively encounter an attacker in each type of environment, but, more importantly, we should think about taking precautionary measures before entering any location. We should learn how to judge an environment by its own physical parameters and, thus, avoid placing ourselves in situations where physical danger is imminent.

The Car and Self-Defense

To begin the study of environmental self-defense, we can begin by viewing the defining factors of the car we use. The car is a common place where confrontations take place, because road rage is so prevalent. Many people are in and out of the car in parking lots late at night—or even during the day. It is a very important physical environment to master in environmental self-defense.

For example, if an attacker rushes toward you, while you are still in the car, if you attempt to get out, you are leaving yourself highly prone to attack. Not only must you get up out of your seat and turn to face the opponent (in which case he or she can easily strike you to the back or side of your head before you can confront the attacker), but you must also open the car door and expose at least one leg before you can even stand up. With your legs on the ground and your body not yet standing, the attacker has the advantage, and can powerfully smash the car door against your exposed extremities. There is virtually nothing you can do to halt this type of attack except to—hopefully—overpower the attacker's superior position, and either get out of the car or get your legs back into the car. By this time, you are probably injured and your self-defense options are highly limited.

Therefore, it is very important to fully evaluate your environment before beginning to leave the car pending a confrontation. If an attacker has already rushed the car, don't attempt to get out—lock the doors, close the windows, drive away! Forget the anger that led to this unsavory situation.

We could be approached by a potential assailant as we attempt to get into the car—and here the car, itself, can be an impeding factor to keep the attacker at bay. If we see an attacker approaching, we can keep the car between us. If he or she begins to move around it, we move in the opposite direction! Though this may look like a child's game, by forcing the assailant to remain at a distance, we can ascertain his or her intentions and hopefully call other people who are in the area to our aid.

If, out of frustration, the attacker attempts to supersede our movements and jumps over the hood or trunk of the car, this is the ideal time to deliver a powerful first strike as he or she is coming off the car. He or she will be off balance due to exaggerated movements, and will be open to any striking technique.

Outdoors

In any physical confrontation that takes place outdoors, we possess a very important advantage for effective self-defense. That advantage is space. In an outdoor situation, we can move if we are accosted. This does not necessarily mean that we should run, though this may be our best defense. What it does mean, however, is that we are not required to stay boxed in a stationary location, as is the case with interior combat.

An attacker rushes in, and by moving backward or sideways, out of his path of attack, his initial offense is foiled. At this point we can launch a powerful counterattack, or just quickly leave the site of the altercation altogether.

When defending yourself from an attack that happens outdoors, the most important thing to keep in mind is to keep moving. Each time the assailant attempts to punch, step back out of his path of attack. If he attempts to grab, move away. If he does take hold of your body or clothing, immediately free yourself from his grasp, in the most elementary way possibly, usually just by rapidly pulling free. Thus, he will not have the opportunity to substantiate his grasp.

Just remember that any attacker is highly adrenalized. As such, his energy is quickly expended. As long as we can keep him away from us, he will be burning excessive amounts of energy and we, remaining relatively calm, will maintain our energy surplus. Thus, like the competent boxer who allows his opponent to chase him around the ring, we can also conserve our energy and counterattack when the opponent is worn out and drained.

The Alley

It is often said that we should back ourselves up against a wall if we are attacked in an outdoor location. This is especially the case if we find ourselves in a narrow outdoor placement, such as an alley. The belief is that by backing up to a wall, the attacker or attackers cannot come around behind us. Though there is a logic to this form of self-defense, the biggest downside to it is that once against a wall, our movements are highly limited and our attackers can close in and strike with multiple assaults. Additionally, our defensive blocking techniques are highly restricted, for with our backs against a wall, we can only move effectively from side to side. If we attempt to push out from the wall, we then must meet the blows of our attackers head on.

For these reasons, moving against a wall should only be employed when it is to some advantage. This situation would occur when the attacker is rapidly rushing in at us. Then, by side-stepping his attack, redirecting his aggressive energy, and guiding his face or body into the wall, we will save ourselves the necessity of forcefully striking out at him—as we have used his own force to cause him to powerfully impact the nearby wall.

In virtually all other cases, it is to our advantage to keep moving if we find ourselves threatened in a walled outdoor location. Even if our movements must be linear, due to the confined configuration of the space, the attackers will still need to chase after us to grab or strike.

Let's consider the attack scenario when the initial altercation occurs and our backs are already against the wall. In these cases, immediately strike a vital point on the attacker—his knees, groin, throat, eyes, temples, and so on. Once this has been accomplished, immediately move off the wall. From this rapid style of self-defense, we may have foiled the attacker's intentions. If not, additional self-defense can be employed as necessary.

The ATM

Automated Teller Machines (ATMs) have become a very common place for individuals with ill intent to accost would-be victims. Though most ATMs now have video surveillance, this has not seemed to halt these attacks, as criminals know it takes several minutes for police to arrive. During this time period they can rob their victims and in some cases injure or kill them. Knowing this, we must all be very cautious whenever using an ATM.

The obvious first line of ATM self-defense is to only go to those located at indoor locations, such as in supermarkets, convenience stores, shopping malls, and so on. If this is not practical, use an ATM in a well-lighted, highly populated outdoor location.

The second level of ATM self-defense, even at the previously described inhabited locations, is to witness your environment thoroughly. Visually scan the entire area for shady-looking individuals before you get out of your car or walk up to the ATM machine. If you see an individual who looks out of place, never give that person the benefit of the doubt, as it may cost you your life. Instead, leave the location, go find another, potentially safer ATM.

At times, you may have viewed the area and surmised that there was no apparent danger. As you are beginning your ATM transaction, someone walks up behind you. Many ATMs now have mirrors so you can see the approach of other people. These are an important tool of ATM self-defense.

FACE-TO-FACE

One of the primary fundamentals to successful self-defense is to encounter any aggressive individual face-to-face. With this, you can quickly ascertain his or her intentions and see if an attack is imminent. For example, if you are alone at an ATM, and someone comes up behind you, immediately turn around to face that person. If it turns out that he or she is only waiting to use the machine, smile and all will be well. If, on the other hand, he intends to rob you, then your self-defense can instantly begin, and you will have a better chance to counterattack his vital strike points and emerge victorious.

Your Money or Your Life

An important factor to calculate into any self-defense scenario is the following: if all the person accosting you wants is money or jewelry, give it to him! Too many people have died needlessly, attempting to fight over a few dollars that can be replaced. Though being robbed is certainly not just, dying unnecessarily because of a robbery serves absolutely no purpose.

The other case to consider is that many attackers possess no value for human life and may take your money and then injure you, as well. In these situations you must defend yourself to your utmost, defeating them by any means necessary.

BUS STOPS AND SUBWAY STATIONS

Many people travel by means of public transportation. Whether this is motivated by environmental consciousness or due to financial constraints, locations such as bus stops and subway stations have long been a hotbed of criminal activity. This is primarily due to the fact that potential victims are there waiting. Thus, they are not only available but are easily accessible stationary targets.

For obvious time-constraint reasons, you may not always be able to walk away from a location of public transportation once you have arrived. If this is your case and you must remain, even though you have taken notice of potential danger, you possess two possible means of initial self-defense. The first is to stand back in a position where the suspicious person or persons cannot see you. Once the bus or subway train pulls up, rapidly move toward it and get on—where other people are hopefully present. You must keep in mind, however, that no matter how much in a hurry you are, you do not want to enter an enclosed location if you and your suspicious counterpart are the only people present. This may leave you open for a confrontation with no one to come to your aid. If this is your situation, do not board the public transportation. Let the suspicious individual get on, and wait for the next bus or train to arrive. With the simple action of waiting you have not given your potential attacker the opportunity to take advantage of you.

The second means of preemptive public transportation self-defense is in direct contrast to the first. As has often times been proven, assailants often work in teams. You may see the first one, but his associates may be laying in wait. If you retreat to the shadows, that may be exactly where they want you. For this reason, staying in the open may be the most efficient way to encounter your potential assailants. With this action you present a presence of no fear. If they begin to move in your direction, you have a better chance to rapidly leave the environment or, if necessary, encounter them face-to-face.

As is the case with all self-defense situations, it is you who must study your environment and make the most appropriate choice to assure your safety.

Stealth Mode

An important first step in environmental self-defense is that when you enter a new location, you do so in what can be called the "Stealth Mode." In other words, do not flamboyantly walk in, see trouble, turn, and leave. If you have entered a location and a criminal has taken notice of you, he or she may well follow your exit. For this reason, study the environment with each step you quietly take as you move toward it. See everything before it has the opportunity to see you.

Waiting

When you are awaiting public transportation, placing yourself in a well-lighted, populated spot is clearly your first choice. You must keep in mind, however, that many crimes take place while bystanders watch and do nothing. This is a sad fact of modern society. Though screaming and asking for help is appropriate, you must immediately launch into your own self-defense if you are accosted, even in a public place, as this may be your only chance to defeat an attacker.

NIGHTCLUBS AND BARS

Nightclubs and bars are familiar focal points for social interaction. Designed to be lighthearted places of enjoyment, they nonetheless are environments where physical altercations take place. Whether this is due to the alcohol consumption common to these locations, or simply based on the fact that people regress to animalistic tendencies when they socialize, these are places where your physical self-defense abilities may be put to the test.

Certainly, from a wholly spiritual perspective, we could say that these locations should not be frequented destinations at all, as they provoke a less than savory mind-set, and the people we tend to encounter there are focused more prominently upon self-gratification than enlightenment. From a more realistic standpoint, however, we all seek human interaction. Thus, it is not uncommon, no matter what our metaphysical makeup, to avail ourselves of these establishments.

It's fun! Therefore, when we meet a friend to share a beer to celebrate a new promotion, we might want to be aware that we are not the center of the universe. Some common sense needs to come with us to the celebration, and it's important to be aware that an angry, frustrated person might enter into our world. So while we celebrate, we should stay aware.

Being intoxicated, even slightly, is never to your advantage if you must defend yourself. As is common knowledge, alcohol quickly causes loss of the balance and coordination that are both essential in all self-defense applications. Therefore, while drinking alcohol in nightclubs and bars is common, your first, and most recommended step, when relating the science of self-defense to these locations, is to replace alcohol with soft drinks, club soda, or mineral water. By doing this, not only will you maintain your physical equilibrium, but you will hold fast to your mental presence, as well. If accosted, you will be ready.

It is not uncommon for an intoxicated individual to come up to you in a bar and attempt to instigate a confrontation for any number of irrational reasons. As is the case with all meaningless physical encounters, it is best to just walk away and let the instigator say what he will— as words emanating from the mouths of those who choose to exist at the low levels of confrontationally based existence should mean nothing to you. If the person forces an altercation, and you have no other way to assure your safety but to defend yourself, you must ideally strike first. You go for one of his or her vital points, and debilitate the person with rapid and decisive blows. Once you have done this, you must leave the site of the altercation immediately, as aggressors in these locations are generally never alone.

Furthermore, if you allow the altercation to digress into a grappling match, you will no doubt be confronted by a "bouncer," who certainly won't care who started the fight, and who will forcefully dispatch both of you from the venue! From this, you may become injured and the altercation may continue on the street.

The other element that must be considered is the scenario where an individual waits for you outside the nightclub or bar. Again, this may be stimulated by any number of events. Your best first line of defense is to be very conscious as you *exit any location.* Awareness of an oncoming confrontation is essential to your assured victory. Thus, you should never lackadaisically exit an environment, leaving to chance what may or may not occur.

If you notice that someone is waiting for you, alert the staff of the establishment. If staff will not help you, call law enforcement. They will come to the scene most of the time. It is essential that you never let your ego supersede your safety. Never believe that you are so tough you don't need to ask for help.

Remember, you don't want to sink to the level of unconscious confrontation. You should only be willing to enter into a physical confrontation if it is absolutely necessary for your immediate safety, or for the safety of someone else. To this end, whatever it takes to restrain the aggression without fighting, reach out to those sources and ask for help. This may be a bouncer, a doorman, a policeman, or other people who will back you up if you let them know you need help.

FROM THE UNSEEN

If, while leaving a nightclub or bar, you are attacked from the unseen by people who have been lying in wait, don't try to go head-to-head with them by exchanging blows. As the aggressors possess the advantage of numbers, this will never be to your advantage.

When dealing with multiple opponents, the best thing you can do is to strike a vital point on one of your attackers and quickly retreat—preferably to a location where other people are in attendance and you can call for help.

When you go to a nightclub or bar, assuredly you are not going there seeking trouble. Unfortunately, this is not the case with everyone. Physical attacks that start in or near these establishments are no longer limited to simple bar fights. New forms of assault have come into existence in recent times—among them frightening drugs, such as Rohypnol (commonly known as "ruffies") that, when introduced to someone's drink, causes a virtual coma for several hours. It has been documented that, under the influence of this drug, many people have been assaulted and wake remembering little or nothing from the experience. People have been robbed and brutalized; women have been sexually assaulted and don't know what happened.

Certainly, you must keep very close tabs on what you put into your body in these places. No longer can you leave a drink sitting on a table or bar, go and dance, return, and trust that it will be the same drink that you left on the table.

More than simply being conscious of your drinks and your surroundings, it is essential that you avoid frequenting these locations alone. Go with friends who will watch over you and protect you from being semiconsciously led away. With friends in attendance, you will at least be assured of possessing a first line of defense, if you are accosted physically or in a devious manner.

FOR WOMEN ONLY

It is a biological fact that, in most cases, men are physically stronger than women. In addition, due to the structure of society, men are more physical growing up. They fought with friends and with bullies just to survive school. Young women, on the other hand, are much less likely to go hand-to-hand with their classmates, although some do. From the experience of physical confrontations, men developed the understanding of what it feels like to be hit. Women do not commonly possess this knowledge. Therefore, most females are not as prepared for the realm of physical combat as are their male counterparts.

These two primary factors have led to untold indiscretions, at the hands of unenlightened males, against females who have been forcefully overpowered to no justifiable end other than that of masculine dominance. This being said, it does not mean that women must walk through life scared, though it is wise to be apprehensive of unknown men and unfamiliar locations. If a woman is accosted by a man, she must never attempt to fight him strength against strength. Instead, her self-defense must be unleashed in a much more refined manner.

Words—The First Step

It is not unusual for men to approach women virtually anywhere and attempt to make contact. Most men are understanding when a woman doesn't wish to carry on a conversation. There are some men, however, who possess such a low sense of self-esteem that they become offended if the woman does not immediately respond to them. For this reason, a woman must be cautious about her reaction to any man who approaches her. It is not fair, but it is a fact of life.

Common courtesy prescribes that it is best to encounter all of humanity with a cordial demeanor. It is understandable that a woman may dismiss unwelcome advances from a man in a rude fashion. Even though the man may deserve this type of treatment, it sets the stage for confrontation.

Many altercations are won simply by being nice and then quickly removing yourself from the location. This is especially true when being approached by an unknown male. Be nice, say, "Excuse me, I must go," and leave. From this style of behavior, no one was unnecessarily offended, and you are free to go on your way.

The adverse to this easy exit occurs when a potentially dangerous individual is dismissed by means of insult. To the insecure or mentally unstable, this may be seen as justification for becoming abusive and aggressive. Therefore, it is best to keep your opinions in check and not become invective without provocation.

If a male accosts you and is obviously not going to take "no" for an answer, it is far better to call others to your aid than to enter into a verbal confrontation with him. There are some men who actually enjoy the invigoration of a women who is protesting. Thus, it will do you little good.

Let's Get Physical

Many women are very uncomfortable about hurting another person— even an attacker. Due to this psychological makeup, some women, even while being attacked, are reluctant to believe that it is happening to them and that they must fight back. Though this is certainly a sign of humanity, all humanistic ideology must be put aside if you are physically attacked by an aggressive assailant!

No one can make you think in a defensive manner if you choose not to do so. For this reason, it is you who *must* refine your understanding of how you interact with the human race to the degree that you *will* take defensive action, physical if need be, to protect yourself and those you love from the advances of an assailant.

If a man grabs you while you are dismissing his advances, it is essential that you rapidly apply disengaging techniques (some of which are detailed in later chapters of this book), in association with loudly and sternly saying, "No." This will free you, as well as bring attention to your situation, which will hopefully cause others to come to your aid.

At times, there may be no other people in the vicinity when a person with ill intent attempts to physically take control of you. As in all cases of self-defense, the moment this occurs is the time when you must immediately deliver a powerful strike to one of his vital points—with the most devastating blow you can unleash. Just because there may be no one else around at the time of the altercation, don't think that you can't yell! Just as the martial artist lets out a yell in association with his offensive or defensive maneuver, signifying the expelling of chi energy, you, too, can use the yell as a weapon of self-defense. A yell, used in association with your defensive technique, may distract your attacker, even if only momentarily. This allows you to deliver a well-placed debilitating strike to one of his vital points.

One on One

If a man is attempting to overpower you and force himself upon you, it is essential to immediately take decisive action. When you strike out, these hits are ideally targeted at his groin. Don't limit your self-defense to hand, knee, or leg strikes, however. If an assault is in progress, powerfully grabbing his groin region with your hand will cause immense pain. If reaching this region is impractical, bite any location of his body and don't let go—or, gouge his eyes with your fingers!

It is essential to remember that it doesn't matter how pretty your self-defense technique looks, only that you remove yourself from the grasp of your attacker. Once your initial counterattack has been unleashed, don't wait to witness the results. The moment when you substantially inflict pain is when your attacker is most vulnerable. This is your time to slip from his grasp and escape.

No Random Strikes

Don't randomly strike at your attacker, or attempt to hit him in a non-decisive manner. As I said, most men possess the ability to weather these types of attacks. In fact, by attempting to defend yourself in this fashion, you may aggravate your attacker, causing him to become more adrenalized. If this happens, even your well-placed blows will prove to be less effective. Furthermore, by striking randomly you will quickly tire yourself out. This is certainly not to your advantage in a self-defense situation. Therefore, hold on to your senses and use only well-placed and strongly delivered strikes or counterattack maneuvers, ideally delivered to body locations assured to cause your attacker immense pain so he will cease his assault. Even if this lasts for only a moment, it will give you the opportunity to escape, to call for help, or to grab some object to aid in your self-defense.

ENVIRONMENTAL DETERMINANTS

As a savvy self-defense technician, male or female, you learn to use the environment to your own defensive advantage. Make all landscape and physical objects your ally. Use the environment to help you emerge unscathed from a physical altercation.

There are numerous environmental determinants that should be evaluated if you find yourself in an outdoor confrontation. For example, are you on a hill? If you find yourself on a hill, it is to your advantage to place yourself in the higher stance, above your opponent. From this, you will possess the superior positioning, where he must travel uphill to you. Powerful, low level kicks can be effortlessly unleashed at him from this position. You have easy access to his head and upper body region. This upper positioning is also important if a confrontation is taking place on stairs.

If you find yourself at the lower level in the encounter, and exchanging places with your attacker is not possible, then your best strategy is to move downhill, away from him, and make him come to you. As he will be required to move in a descending fashion, he will be off balance. You can take advantage of this by striking him with a powerful punch to his groin, knee, or shin as he moves in on you. You can, additionally, quickly take him from his feet by grasping his forward leg, at ankle level, and rapidly pulling it downhill toward you. Once he is on the ground, a secondary counterattack can be successfully unleashed.

A similar style of movement-oriented environmental fighting can take place inside buildings, such as bars or rooms where you have space to move. Though you are much more confined in these interior locations, by continually moving away from your attacker, not only does he become drained of energy, but he may become frustrated, as well. A frustrated attacker is easily disabled.

If you find yourself engaged in a close-contact indoor-fighting situation, and movement cannot be your first line of self-defense, then immediately striking your attacker at one of his vital points is a viable first line of defense. These strikes can be substantially aided by picking up any nearby object, such as a bottle, a glass, or anything with weight, and striking him in the head with it. Though this may seem less than sporting, if you are being attacked by an unknown assailant, your survival is the only desired outcome. Thus, protect yourself by any means necessary.

Available Weaponry

One of the key factors to environmental self-defense is to use anything at your disposal to secure your victory in the confrontation. As you did not instigate the fight, there should never be a second thought about this process.

There are many objects at your self-defense disposal if you are targeted by an attacker. Your backpack or purse can be used to hit him. The hot coffee from your cup can be thrown in his face. Put your keys between your fingers and punch him. Your credit or ATM card can be used for slashing across an attacker's face. Sand or dirt from the ground can be picked up and thrown in your attacker's eyes. Doors can be closed on his arms. You can retreat behind doorways, concealing your oncoming punch. Nearby flashlights, lamps, pipes, boards, or trash-can lids can be used to block or strike. Even a rolled up newspaper can be used to strike at an attacker, momentarily startling him as you launch a counterattack.

In all self-defense situations, use the environment to your advantage. Train yourself, as you walk down streets or enter unknown rooms, to study any elements at hand that could be used to aid in your defense. See all landscapes and objects as friendly helpers to keep you safe.

SELF-DEFENSE IS YOU

Many people, men and women alike, have found themselves in situations they did not believe would become confrontational or violent. This end result may be based in trust, naïveté, or simple stupidity. No matter what the cause, the moment you are face-to-face with your own survival, you will realize that all factors of causation and the thoughts of, "You knew better . . ." have no meaning.

It cannot be emphasized enough that it is you who must take responsibility for the situations in which you find yourself. Nobody can think for you or make you aware of your social and physical environment if you refuse to take notice. You certainly cannot control all of life. You may end up in a less than savory environment if, for example, your car breaks down. But, the majority of situations you do have control over. You must make the conscious decision to keep yourself safe!

Many individuals, due to infatuation with a person, a desire for experience, or peer pressure, end up in confrontational encounters that did not have to happen. *You* have the ability to avoid these events by making the choice not to be alone with an unknown individual or on uncharted ground that may prove unsafe.

In the previous pages I have presented some self-defense scenarios, which hopefully will keep you separated from battle, or may help you if you are physically attacked. On the pages that follow, there are direct how-to techniques that, if practiced, may help you to defend yourself. It must be completely understood, however, that there is no end-all method of self-defense. All you can do is be as aware as possible and attempt to make conscious decisions each moment of your life.

Self-defense consciousness is your responsibility. No one can make you aware of your environment if you do not choose to look around you. Nobody can make you defend yourself if you live in fear. For these reasons, you must look to yourself and consciously become a competent self-defense technician. This involves, perhaps more than anything else, listening to your inner voice before you enter any life situation. "Is this the right thing to be doing?" "Is this the right place to be?" If you have doubt, that doubt is your self-defense teacher. Leave!

If you find yourself in an altercation and physical battle is your only means of protection, listen to your inner voice. This is the nature of the martial arts—you allow yourself to become naturally reactive in matters of self-defense.

Remember, you are your first line of defense. Move through life consciously.

Self-Defense Principles

There is only virtue in non-stagnation.
People get fixed at one point, with the result that they become
unaware of what came before or what is to come after.
These people lack virtue.

—SHOSAN SUZUKI

Fluidity of movement and the unstoppable profound progression of nature are the key precepts of the martial arts and the enlightened being. Stagnation means you have become immobile. Just as the child's movements are free flowing, and the old person becomes stiff with age, you must embrace the flowingness of the river, encountering, but never stopping. The movements of your life are like the wind—potentially destructive, but more often gently caressing.

To begin to master the complexities of self-defense, you must understand that there is no definition on the streets. You have no idea what an attacker may launch at you. For this reason, if you are attacked, you must make your counter-defensive actions very quickly and very powerfully. To accomplish this, you must discard all the noneffective defensive techniques you may have learned in a martial arts school or a self-defense class, and redefine the techniques that are truly effective against each kind of attack that may occur—be it a punch, kick, choke hold, or knife stab.

To become an effective self-defense technician, you must make self-defense a science. You must understand why certain techniques and their applications are superior and more effective than others. Through this knowledge, you come to truly understand the Science of Self-Defense. And you need to practice this and think about this now, as you won't have time to think about it when you are being attacked!

THE MOTION PHILOSOPHY OF SELF-DEFENSE

The motion philosophy of self-defense is based on six precepts. From them you will learn the ideology of how to emerge unscathed from all types of physical altercations.

1. *Keep your defensive techniques simple*
Discard in theory and practice overly elaborate striking, blocking, disengaging, grappling, or throwing techniques. Self-defense techniques, to be effective, must be very fast and very easy.

2. *Continuous motion*
Once you have been engaged in combat, keep all self-defense techniques, be they defensive or offensive, flowing continually from one onto the next. Never stop until you have defeated your attacker.

3. *Strike first*
If attack is imminent and there is nothing you can do to get away from the confrontation, strike fast and strike hard. From this, the confrontation will end before you have the potential of becoming injured.

4. *Counterstrike*
Immediately upon disengaging any hold, or instantly upon moving out

of the path of an adversary's attack, strike before the attacker has the opportunity to realign his energies and launch a secondary attack.

5. *Use your attacker's own energy against himself*
When an attacker launches an assault, step out of its path and use his own aggressive momentum to aid you in your self-defense.

6. *Range effectiveness*
All self-defense techniques, be they offensive or defensive, must be easily applied. If you have to reach to strike an attacker, he is too far away. Thus, you leave yourself open for counterattacks. Let an attacker move to you.

The practice and application of the six precepts of the motion philosophy of self-defense will be detailed in the chapters that follow. Through practicing the techniques outlined in this book you will be able to define for yourself a method of self-defense that will allow you to emerge victorious from any form of attack.

THE DYNAMICS OF CONTINUOUS MOTION

The Theory of Continuous Motion is the most important understanding you can embrace to become an effective self-defense technician. The Theory of Continuous Motion teaches that you establish a continuum from one self-defense technique onto the next, and to the next, until your attacker has no chance of recovering and launching a secondary assault upon you. There are three rules of continuous motion.

1. Never expect that your initial block, deflection, or counterstrike will be enough to disable your attacker.

2. Any technique you unleash must possess the structure to be quickly re-formed and re-directed.

3. If you lock yourself too tightly into a single maneuver you will not be able to quickly redirect it if your attacker moves or launches an unexpected secondary attack.

It is common in self-defense training to follow a block with a punch; a punch with a kick, and so on. This is all too stylized, however, and street altercations are never like that. It is very clear to anyone who has ever been involved in a fight that disengaging a hold or deflecting a punch and then counterattacking with a single offensive technique is virtually never enough to emerge victorious from the confrontation. It is doubtful that you will possess the ability to strike with enough force to completely disable your attacker in a single blow. Even if you send him to the ground with a well-placed punch, kick, or throw, he has the potential to recover and again come after you. Therefore, the theory of continuous motion teaches you how to effortlessly flow from one self-defense technique onto the next until your opponent is completely disabled.

In a physical encounter you must never believe that the single offensive technique you have unleashed will make debilitating contact with your attacker. Engulfed in battle, people are constantly in motion—they move. This is especially the case with a trained fighter who sees an oncoming assault.

Many traditional martial arts systems teach students to lock into a formal stance and then unleash a forceful technique. Anything that you do to alert your opponent to the fact that an offensive strike is impending provides the attacker with the time to ready his defenses. For this reason, you can't signal your offensive assaults by entering into a formal stance or overtly taking aim with your fists or your feet. Instead, keep your self-defense allusive by never making any distinctive movements until your technique is traveling toward the other person's body.

While in combat, your opponent will be in motion. Though he may not do so from a refined understanding of continuous motion, he, nonetheless, will be jockeying for superior positioning. To this end, never lock yourself into one technique. If he moves, change your pattern of counterattack and strike in another manner that will still make contact. Keep your arms, hands, feet, and legs loose, so you can change your offensive or defensive strategy instantly, and redirect or restructure any form of your self-defense.

Striking Techniques

It is far more wise to stop before you fill to the top.

If you over-sharpen a blade—the edge will soon be dull.

If you amass a store of wealth and power, no army

can protect it.

—LAO TZU

The modern world breeds a consciousness that each individual possesses the right to walk over anyone in order to obtain his or her desires. There have, in fact, been positive titles given to these people: they are driven, motivated, or goal seekers. The sad thing about this mentality is that personal victory is seldom good for the rest of humanity. The person who "wins" wants something for personal reasons and often believes these personal desires are the only right desires for the whole of mankind.

The people who exist at this level of being walk on the razor's edge. They are tense, edgy, and have little control over their emotions. They are controlled by the desire to win all confrontations and expound their power and ideology in any and all situations.

How can you combat this mentality? Do not enter into battle with them at any level. By not allowing your mind and body to be lured into confrontation, you are free—the desires another possesses do not control you. Thus, you can easily walk away.

Delivering First Strikes

When your opponent is startled and his feelings are distracted—
your opponent will experience a gap in reaction time.

—YAGYU MUNENORI

This gap in opponent consciousness is what all refined warriors look for while emerged in the grasp of battle. This is the moment when the adversary has been distracted. If this distraction exists—even for a second in time—refined warriors will use it to their own advantage and strike their adversary's weakest, most vulnerable point. With this style of physical or mental warfare, battles are quickly won and they do not continue for an unnecessary length of time.

To begin your development of essential self-defense, you must first and foremost understand that no confrontation is ever won by a long exchange of punches or kicks. A street fight is commonly won or lost in the first few seconds of the altercation, and it is generally the first strike that targets a vital point which sets the stage for victory.

Vital strike points are defined as locations on the body that, when impacted, cause an individual pain to the degree that he or she will be stopped from continuing forward with the attack. In this instance, you

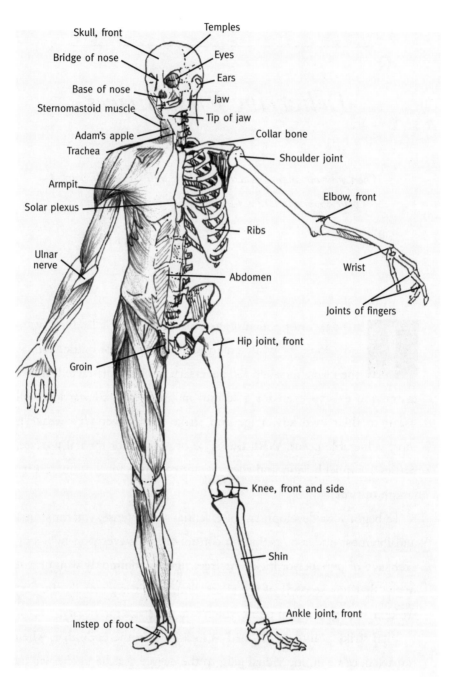

Skull, front
Temples
Bridge of nose
Eyes
Base of nose
Ears
Sternomastoid muscle
Jaw
Tip of jaw
Adam's apple
Collar bone
Trachea
Shoulder joint
Armpit
Elbow, front
Solar plexus
Ribs
Ulnar nerve
Wrist
Abdomen
Joints of fingers
Hip joint, front
Groin
Knee, front and side
Shin
Ankle joint, front
Instep of foot

Basic Front Attack Locations

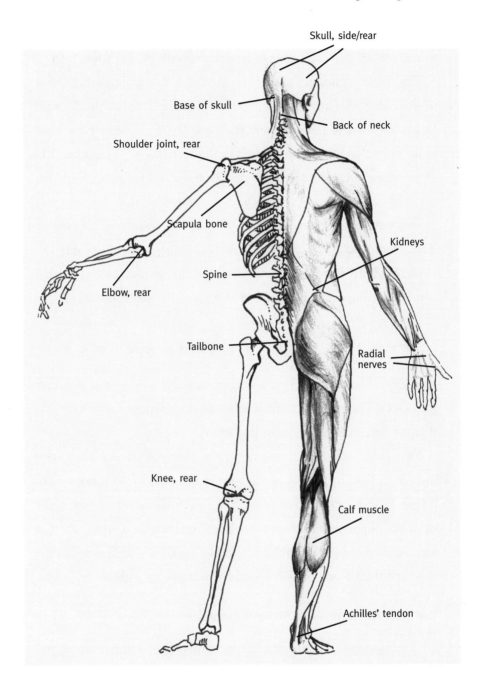

Basic Rear Attack Locations

have the ability to either leave the scene of the confrontation or unleash secondary self-defense tactics to ensure your victory over your attacker.

The most common location to go for is the male groin. Other obvious locations are located on the head: the temples, the forward throat, the base of the nose, and the eyes. There are many other vital strike points on the human body. The illustrations on pages 38 and 39 show where an individual can be hit and debilitated. Though the majority of these require a more well-defined strike than does the previously detailed vital strike points, they are all equally viable targets. Throughout this book you will learn techniques that will enable you to successfully target all these strike points so you can apply the appropriate impact to interrupt or halt any adversary's attack.

FIRST STRIKE ADVANTAGE

Applying a focused attack to a vital strike point is what sets the stage for victory. Therefore, the initial lesson in the science of self-defense is that the first strike is the most important.

First strike advantage does not mean that you should go up and instigate a fight by punching someone in the face. What it does mean is that the moment you find yourself in a confrontation, you powerfully strike your opponent in the most debilitating location on the body that you can easily reach. From this you gain a substantial defensive advantage, and the altercation will hopefully continue no further.

The Four Rules of First Strike Advantage

1. The moment a hostile attacker encounters you, or the moment you are grabbed, is the moment to strike.

2. Strike your attacker in the most debilitating location on the body before he or she has the ability to overpower you.

3. Strike your attacker with the part of your body that will cause the most damage with the least amount of effort.

4. Do not reach, stretch, or overextend yourself when you attempt the first strike, for this leaves you prone to counterattack.

Any strike you make must be fast, easy, and have the potential to instantly debilitate your attacker. All elaborate punching, kicking, and striking techniques you have learned in "school" should be left there. For though they may be pretty to practice and watch in a controlled environment, they are useless against a competent street fighter.

Any part of your body can be used as a weapon—your fists, elbows, knees, feet, and even your head are all viable tools. How do you determine the part of your body to use in combat? Use the one that is the easiest to unleash and the most devastating to your attacker.

Deploying Your Hands and Arms

There are many who believe that practicing the martial arts is not
useful because when the time arrives they will not be able to utilize the
skills necessary to defeat an opponent. The true way to practice the martial
arts is in such a way that they will be useful in any circumstance.

—MIYAMOTO MUSASHI

Many systems of self-defense are unnecessarily elaborate in both philosophic scope and physical technique, though the demonstration of these systems may be very beautiful to observe. When practitioners of these systems find themselves engaged in battle, they become mentally confused when determining the technique to use and find that their physical defenses are quickly overpowered by their opponents, who are not bound by any formal structure.

Free yourself of unnecessary philosophy in battle.
Keep your techniques simple and direct.
You will emerge victorious.

It is a natural practice to begin to defend yourself with your hands and fists if you are engaged in an unexpected battle. Therefore, it is imperative that you know how to use your hands and fists in the most effective manner. To this end, we will begin by viewing effective offensive techniques that employ your hands and your arms.

THE FIGHTING STANCE

A fighting stance is common to all forms of self-defense. Whether developed through traditional martial arts or boxing classes, or simply the stance you take when a confrontation is imminent, it is basically the same.

The fighting stance witnesses a person standing with legs naturally apart, maintaining a natural balance. The elbows are traditionally bent at a 45-degree (or greater) angle, and are suspended at mid-torso, a few inches away from the body. The hands are formed into fists. One arm, referred to as the "lead arm," is generally higher, and somewhat out in front of the other arm. The rear arm maintains a rear protective positioning. (See figure 1.)

In discussing the offensive techniques that follow, it will be assumed that they will be launched from a fighting stance. Certainly, all self-defense situations are different. Do not believe that to effectively strike an attacker you must remain in a traditional stance. You may alter the fighting stance, as necessary, to make your individual techniques most effective.

THE STRAIGHT PUNCH

The Straight Punch is a highly linear offensive technique. In a Straight Punch, your fist is launched from your shoulder and is directed straight toward its target, with your fist horizontal to the ground. The Straight Punch is ideally delivered when the elbow of your punching arm remains slightly bent upon making impact with its target. This is accomplished by accurately judging the distance and hitting your objective

before your arm reaches the point where it must stretch or extend unnaturally to reach the desired strike point. By allowing your elbow to remain slightly bent whenever you use a Straight Punch, you not only maintain maximum body balance, but you also keep your elbow from possible hyperextension, as the momentum of the punch drives it forward.

The primary element that gives the Straight Punch its devastating power is the fact that you make contact with your target before you have fully extended your punching arm. If your Straight Punch reaches its target as close to its point of inception as possible, this allows you to continue forward with the force and power of the punch, extending it deeply into your opponent. If, on the other hand, you have to reach to make contact with your opponent, you will have expended a large portion of the power of your punch before it ever impacts its target. (See figure 2 on page 45.)

The Straight Punch Versus the Roundhouse Punch

The reason the Straight Punch is the preferred punching technique for self-defense applications is due to the fact that it is exceedingly fast and difficult to defend. As such, it holds several advantages over the more common Roundhouse Punch. For example, the Roundhouse Punch is delivered by the punching arm first swinging outward and then in toward its target. Due to its design, the Roundhouse Punch is not only much slower than the Straight Punch, but it is much more obvious and easily defended against.

In the wildly agitated combat that takes place in a street altercation, the Straight Punch is one of your best first-line defenses. As your opponent prepares to launch his attack or wildly swing his arms attempting to hit you, the Straight Punch instantly penetrates virtually any offensive or defensive maneuver. Thus, your adversary is powerfully hit before he has the opportunity to strike you.

THE BACK FIST

The Back Fist is an extremely rapid offensive weapon. To unleash the Back Fist, your elbow is bent and your fist, in a vertical position, is brought back to your chest at shoulder level. The Back Fist is then unleashed at its target by first snapping your elbow out and then extending the distance of the Back Fist's attack from your shoulder. The Back Fist is generally aimed at your opponent's head. (See figure 3 on page 47.)

The Back Fist is difficult to defend against. This is due to the fact that it is a very rapid striking weapon, and once impact is made, your fist is rapidly recoiled. The Back Fist can, therefore, be used multiple times when additional striking measures are necessary.

THE PALM STRIKE

The Palm Strike, like the Straight Punch, is delivered in a linear fashion. The Palm Strike has you bend your fingers at the second knuckle, which exposes the base of your palm. By bending your fingers in this fashion, the muscle that extends from the thumb across the base of your hand is tightened, thus providing a powerful striking weapon. Your palm is then brought back to shoulder level. It is unleashed by snapping the strike toward its target with your shoulder muscles.

The Palm Strike is most effectively used to target locations on your opponent's head, such as underneath the base of the nose (which can prove deadly), across the bridge of the nose, the temples, or the side of the jaw. (See figure 4.)

THE KNIFE HAND

To form the Knife Hand, the fingers are extended and the muscles and tendons in the hand and wrist are tightened. The initial mistake many individuals make when attempting to use the Knife Hand as a weapon is to relax the tension in the hand either just before or during the Knife Hand Strike. This should never be done, for you can easily break bones in your own hand!

The basic strike weapon of the Knife Hand is along the base of the hand. This extends from where the wrist ends to where the little finger begins. The arched side is the location where the Knife Hand possesses the most strength because of the aforementioned tightening techniques.

The Knife Hand Strike is propelled by the extension of the arm and then snapping the elbow. The momentum developed by snapping out the elbow should never be allowed to entirely control your Knife Hand assault. The elbow should remain slightly bent when the Knife Hand technique is delivered, thus maintaining control over your movement.

The Knife Hand is not a randomly effective weapon, such as the fist—which can be allowed to strike virtually anywhere on an opponent's body with the hope of having a cumulative effect. Instead, the Knife Hand is ideally suited to strike very specific locations on an opponent's body—the front of the neck, across the nose, to the temples, and to the side of the ribs.

6A

6B

The Knife Hand is unleashed in one of two ways: overhand and underhand. With the Overhand Knife Hand Strike, your hand is propelled with your palm facing upward. This ideally strikes your opponent's neck or across the nose. (See figure 5 on page 49.)

The Underhand Knife Hand (see figure 6) witnesses your hand traveling to its target with your palm facing the ground. This hand strike is ideal to reach your opponent's throat, nose, or temples. The Knife Hand strike you use is defined solely by your location in relation to your opponent.

THE CIRCLE
HAND

This weapon is formed by separating your thumb from your forefinger, tightening the muscles and tendons of the hand, and striking, in a linear fashion, to the frontal region of an attacker's neck (see figure 7).

THE ELBOW STRIKE

The Elbow Strike is a close contact fighting weapon. The Elbow Strike has two applications: the Forward Elbow Strike and the Rear Elbow Strike.

The Forward Elbow Strike requires that you bend your elbow, exposing the protruding elbow bone at the base of your forearm. This bone is your striking tool. This Elbow Strike is ideally targeted at a vital strike point on your opponent's head.

To perform the Forward Elbow Strike, bring your elbow up to shoulder level and by pivoting your body at waist level, and if possible stepping in with your lead foot, you make impact on your target. The

Forward Elbow Strike is an ideal tool for close contact fighting if you find that your opponent has taken a powerful forward hold on your body and his temples or face are exposed (see figure 8).

The Rear Elbow Strike is an ideal weapon to use if an attacker has grabbed hold of your body from behind. If you have been grabbed from behind, the Rear Elbow Strike requires that you pivot backward, unleashing your bent elbow from shoulder level, making impact on virtually any part of your attacker's body.

If you have not yet been grabbed from behind, but your attacker is close, you can add an additional momentum-driven movement from your body to the strike by pivoting at waist level as your Rear Elbow Strike is unleashed (see figure 9).

Deploying Your Feet

When you see a gate, do not believe that it is the house.
You have to go through the gate to get to the house.
— YAGYU MUNENORI

The people who enter into trivial battles, physical and otherwise, do so based on a superficial consciousness. They are usually driven by an insecure psychological outlook toward life.

A person who is one with the essense of power does not desire power.
An individual who is whole does not desire to control others.

When you are accosted by a power-hungry individual who wants to inflict his or her emotions or ideologies upon you, realize that he or she is only experiencing your external form. Having power over a physical being gives this person misplaced psychological stimulation. It does not mean that this person truly has power over you.

Knowing this, you have already defeated him.

THE KICK

Kicking an attacker is less natural than striking the person with your fists. A kick, however, possesses much more power, due to the fact that the muscles of your legs are much stronger than those of your arms. To this end, with developmental practice, your feet and legs can become highly viable weapons in your self-defense arsenal.

For a kicking technique to be effective as a combat tool, it must be fast, difficult to block, and must proceed to its target in the most efficient manner possible. To this end, the kicking techniques detailed in the following pages meet all the previously described requirements—each serving their own unique purpose and application.

Both legs are used whenever a kicking technique is performed. Your base leg is the leg that balances you and anchors your body to the ground. Your kicking leg is the leg that actually delivers the kick.

The Base Leg

The knee of the base leg should remain slightly bent whenever a kicking technique is performed. This adds to the overall balance of your body, as you will be able to adjust your position by adding more or less bend to your knee to compensate for the height and velocity of your kick. If the knee of your base leg remains locked into a straight up position as you perform any kicking technique, the tendons, cartilage, or the knee itself could easily become damaged.

The Kicking Leg

The kicking leg should never be allowed to fully extend when a kicking technique is performed. The knee of the kicking leg should remain slightly bent. This is accomplished by maintaining muscle control over your leg, thus, not allowing the momentum of the kick to force your knee to extend unnaturally.

The knee joint is one of the most sensitive joints of the body. By keeping the knee of your base leg and your kicking leg slightly bent, you do not allow your knees to hyperextend or bend back, unnaturally, against themselves. Thus, you protect yourself from unnecessary injury.

THE FORWARD (LEAD) LEG KICK

Many traditional martial arts systems launch kicking techniques solely from the rear leg. It is believed that by performing a kick in this fashion the momentum and power of the kick will be substantially increased. Though there is truth to this opinion, by launching a self-defense oriented kicking technique solely from the rear leg, the kick is not only slower, but the kick's travel from inception to target becomes more pronounced. Therefore, an opponent has an increased chance to see it coming and defend against it. For the reason of increased speed and additional overall effectiveness, self-defense oriented kicks can be launched from either the rear or the forward, lead leg—defined only by which will prove most effective. In this way, each of your kicks will have the heightened ability to be tailored to match any self-defense situation.

THE FRONT KICK

The elementary Front Kick is performed by first standing in a traditional fighting stance, with fists clenched in front of you. You then launch your rear leg forward by rapidly raising the knee of your kicking leg up to approximately hip level. The lower section of your kicking leg is then immediately snapped outward in the direction of the target. The Front Kick's power is developed by a combination of upper leg muscle strength and lower leg snapping momentum.

The impact of the Front Kick is made, most effectively, with the ball of your foot. It is essentially important, when front kicking, that your toes be pulled back, even while wearing shoes. If your toes are allowed to remain in their naturally extended position, they can be easily broken when target impact is made. (See figure 10.)

The instep of your foot is a secondary, and highly specific

tool to use in delivering the Front Kick. The instep Front Kick is targeted solely at an opponent's groin, whereas the Front Kick delivered with the ball of the foot can be sent to any body location.

Retracting the Front Kick

Japanese martial arts systems retract the Front Kick with the same snapping speed and velocity as it is delivered; this is not the best way to unleash this technique, as its power is substantially decreased when the leg is retracted as quickly as it is unleashed. Instead, the Front Kick becomes far more powerful when the kicking leg is allowed to remain in position, for a millisecond, in order that the full power of the kick may be delivered to the target.

Focusing the Front Kick

The basic Front Kick is an ideal close contact fighting weapon. It is perfect to unleash against an opponent who has faced off with you and is in very close proximity to your body. As is commonly understood, a Front Kick to the groin is universally debilitating. Other close contact Front Kick targets are the solar plexus, stomach, or under the jaw of your adversary.

The Front Kick, by it very nature, is a very direct, linear kick. It has the ability to readily penetrate your attacker's defenses. It can powerfully shoot in under clenched fists and deliver a powerful blow to the midsection before your attacker even knows what hit him. This could set the stage for your victory in a confrontation.

Front Kick Pitfalls

The beginning practitioner will oftentimes attempt to Front Kick as high into the air as possible. The novice will learn the hard way that if he or she has not yet developed the proper balancing techniques to properly deliver a high Front Kick, when the Front Kick is wildly kicked into the air, the lack of developed balance will send the novice backward onto the ground. Therefore, the Front Kick should be practiced at low levels until it has been mastered.

There is one primary flaw to the basic Front Kick, and that is its range. The basic Front Kick is generally delivered in a vertical motion. The advanced combatant can simply lean back out of the Front Kick's upward driven path of attack and the kick will miss. Therefore, to develop the ability to make the basic Front Kick a truly effective self-defense weapon, it must be slightly redesigned to offer your opponent less ability to easily move from its path. This method is known as the Momentum Driven Front Kick.

THE MOMENTUM-DRIVEN FRONT KICK

Begin in a fighting stance. Prepare to launch a Front Kick from your rear leg. Instead of focusing the power of this kick upward, focus it deeply in toward the solar plexus region of an imaginary opponent who

11A

is standing several feet in front of you. As you unleash your Front Kick, snap your kicking leg outward, allowing the horizontal momentum-driven power of the kick to pull your body forward, sliding your base foot along the ground. Do not attempt to hinder this forward motion. Instead, let it naturally drive you in toward your target. (see figure 11.)

As you practice the Momentum-Driven Front Kick, you will come to realize you can effortlessly travel several feet in toward your opponent without ever losing your balance. This type of front-kicking technique not only gives you additional range, but it gives you additional power, as well, due to the force of your body weight moving in toward your adversary.

Mistakes of the Momentum-Driven Front Kick

The Momentum-Driven Front Kick is a very effective weapon. The leading mistake many people make using this technique is that they extend the snapping motion of their lower leg before they are ever in range of their target. From this, they dissipate the power of the kick before it has had the opportunity to make its impact. Therefore, to make the Momentum-Driven Front Kick a viable offensive technique, you should never extend the lower portion of your leg until you are very close to your target and assured of making contact. If your opponent relocated and the kick will not prove to be effective, you can place the foot of your kicking leg back on the ground and realign yourself for further self-defense.

THE DEFENSIVE FRONT KICK

Due to its effective simplicity, the Front Kick is a very rapid and penetrating offensive weapon. When the Front Kick is employed in defensive applications, you can additionally readily halt any attack launched upon you. The most appropriate opportunity to launch a defensive Front Kick is when your opponent is in the midst of his own offensive action. This is due to the fact that while his offensive technique is in progress, he will not be able to rapidly redirect its motion, nor will he be able to readily block your defensive kick. Thus, he will be in a prone position to meet the full power of your Front Kick.

Deploying the Defensive Front Kick

As an attacker moves in toward you, he begins to swing a Roundhouse Punch in your direction (as shown in figure 12A–B). Before it can strike, use your lead leg to Front Kick him in his midsection. His attack

is instantly halted and you can continue forward with additional self-defense as necessary (see figure 12C).

As you now know, the Front Kick, though very simple to implement, is one of the most effective weapons in your self-defense arsenal. By its very design, the Front Kick can be rapidly delivered, thus saving you from any unnecessarily prolonged confrontation or potential injury.

THE KNEE STRIKE

The Knee Strike is an ideal weapon for close contact self-defense. The Knee Strike is simple to perform—simply raise your knee powerfully up to hip level and strike your opponent with it. The ideal vital strike point is your attacker's groin.

The Knee Strike is ideally used in either an offensive or a defensive application, whenever you are in close proximity to your opponent (see figure 13).

13A   13B

THE SIDE KICK

The basic Side Kick is performed by initially shifting 75 percent of the body weight to your forward base leg as the rear kicking leg rises up with knee bent to waist level. As the kicking leg rises, you pivot on the ball of your base foot 180 degrees—the hip of your kicking leg turns toward its target. Your body leans sideways toward the ground, as your kicking leg is extended toward its target—in a sideways fashion. Impact is made with the heel or outside ridge of your foot.

The Side Kick is ideally targeted at an opponent's knee, stomach, or is delivered by the advanced practitioner, at the opponent's head. (See figure 14.)

Limitations of the Basic Side Kick

The basic Side Kick is launched from the rear leg. This makes it very slow and obvious in combat situations. A trained opponent can easily see it coming and jam or block this kick before you have the opportunity to make contact. For this reason, the basic Side Kick is not always a viable weapon for self-defense. With a few minor alterations, however, the Side Kick can become a very effective tool in your self-defense arsenal.

THE LEAD LEG
SIDE KICK

The traditional Side Kick is launched from the rear leg. To make this same technique more rapid and effective in self-defense applications, you can change this kick's launch point to your front or lead leg.

The Lead Leg Side Kick is implemented by lifting your front, kicking leg up and delivering it to your attacker's knee, stomach, or head in side kick fashion. This Lead Leg Side Kick is especially effective when an attacker is charging in at you. By delivering a side kick to his midsection, not only is his advance immediately halted but he will be stunned and open to further counterattacks as necessary. (See figure 15.)

16A

16B

16C

16D

THE STEPPING SIDE KICK

The Stepping Side Kick is performed by allowing the base leg to rapidly step behind the kicking leg, thus gaining added distance and momentum. The kicking leg is then rapidly extended toward its target in Side Kick fashion.

The Stepping Side Kick is one of the most powerful and effective kicking techniques in your self-defense arsenal. It rapidly penetrates an opponent's defenses. By its design, any bodily location it impacts has the potential to be injured. (See figure 16 on page 68.)

THE ROUNDHOUSE KICK

The traditional Roundhouse Kick is launched from your rear leg. It is directed, in a circular fashion, from its point of origin to its target. This movement is accomplished by pivoting 180 degrees on the ball of the foot of your base leg, as the kick continues to travel toward its goal. (See figure 17 on pages 69 and 70.)

17A

The Roundhouse Kick is a muscle- and momentum-driven weapon. Power is added to it by snapping out your knee just before the kick has reached its impact point. Impact with the Roundhouse Kick is made with the instep of your foot and is ideally directed toward your opponent's knee, thigh, midsection or, by advanced practitioners, at the opponent's head.

THE FORWARD LEG
ROUNDHOUSE KICK

A very effective option of the Roundhouse Kick is to launch it from your forward leg. When the Roundhouse Kick is implemented from this position, its technique is virtually the same, but the momentum-driven body movement is not added to the overall impact. Additionally, when the Roundhouse Kick is launched from the forward leg, it becomes much harder to block. This is based on two factors: first of all, it is much faster, and second, it is harder for your opponent to see it coming. (See figure 18 on pages 71 and 72.)

18A

PART THREE

Deflection and Counterattack Techniques

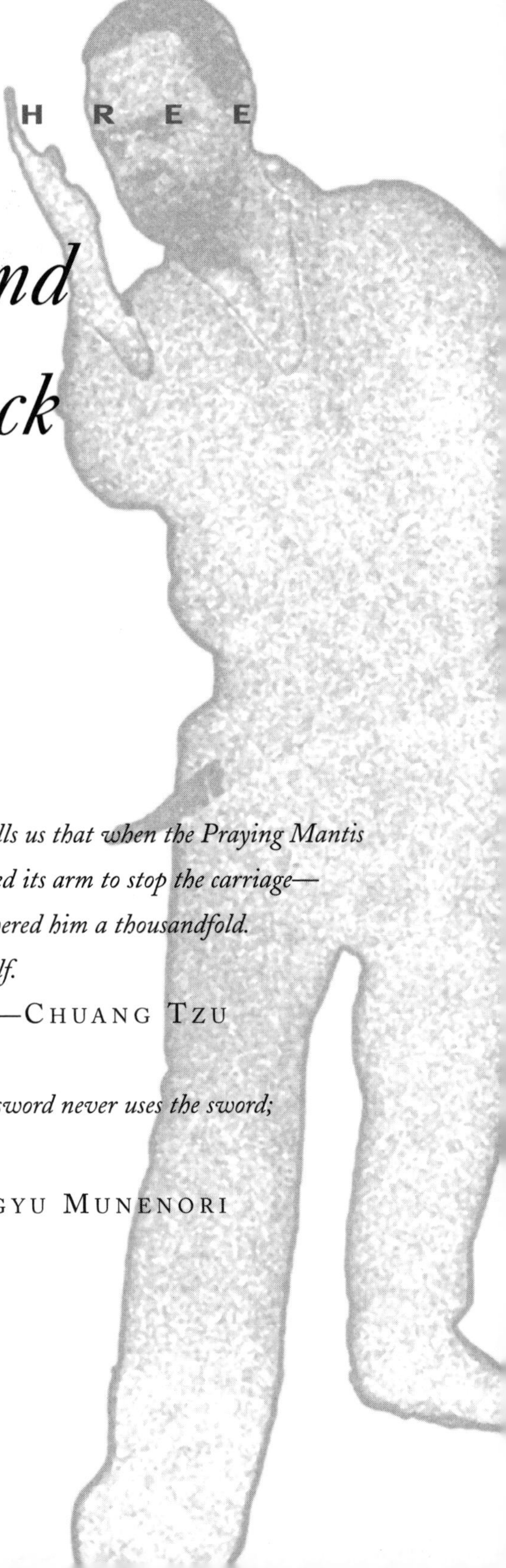

The story of the Praying Mantis tells us that when the Praying Mantis saw a carriage approaching, it raised its arm to stop the carriage— unaware that the carriage overpowered him a thousandfold. Such was his high opinion of himself.

—CHUANG TZU

A man who has fully mastered the sword never uses the sword; he lets the opponent kill himself.

—YAGYU MUNENORI

People who are trained in the various aggressive styles of self-defense are ready to step into verbal or physical confrontations. They do this because they believe—due to the training they possess—that all the skills necessary to defeat any opponent are known and mastered. This is the biggest folly anyone can possess. Encountering any opponent, face-to-face, strength-to-strength is the most unreliable form of self-defense in existence. Never face off with an adversary. Walk away.

If a physical confrontation is unavoidable, let the attacker come to you. From this style of initial self-defense, your adversary's own negative emotions will leave him vulnerable to a powerful and successful counterattack, his own expenditure of energy can be used to take control over his advances, and you can defeat him with his own force.

Controlling the Elbow

Arresting shadows is something you can perform when an
adversary's intentions toward you are perceivable.

—MIYAMOTO MUSASHI

onfrontations have taken place since the dawn of humanity.
No opponent's advances or attacks are new—they have all
been launched before in previous battles. Watch your opponent, study your opponent, observe who he is. With this style of initial
self-defense, you will be able to launch an attack before your adversary
has the ability to unleash his full frontal assault.

As you will attack before he attacks, you will keep his advance in
check. Thus, you have already won the battle.

CONTROLLING YOUR OPPONENT'S ELBOWS

A little known, yet highly regarded, fact of self-defense is that if you
control your opponent's elbow, you virtually control his entire range of
motion.

Elbow Control Exercise

1. Face off with a training partner.

2. Enter into traditional fighting stances.

3. Locate your partner's lead arm elbow.

4. Quickly slide in toward him.

5. Let your lead hand impact the outer region of his elbow.

6. Shove his elbow tightly in against his body.

7. If he retreats backward from this hold, move with him, keeping his elbow locked into his body.

8. If he attempts to turn out of this grasp, apply more pressure and move with him, maintaining control.

This simple elbow control technique controls your opponent so he will not have the ability to strike at you with the arm you control. Additionally, he will have to awkwardly reach his other arm out and around to attempt any type of striking counterattack.

Certainly, this type of elbow control will not maintain indefinite domination over your adversary. What it will effectively achieve, however, is the time needed to effectively keep his offensive movements in check while you continue through with your own self-defense, such as a Straight Punch to his head. (See figure 19 on pages 76 and 77.)

ELBOW CONTROL AND VARIOUS STANCES

The angle your adversary uses to stage his fighting stance is the only variable that must be studied to learn how to effectively take advantage of this virtually effortless initial form of opponent control. In figure 19, a traditional martial arts stance is used.

The Martial Arts Stance

A martial artist will generally hold his or her body in a side angle toward the opponent. In this way, a minimum amount of target is exposed. This martial arts side stance, however, is the easiest to elbow control because the lead elbow is highly exposed.

The Boxing Stance

A boxer or street fighter will generally face off with the central area of the torso facing you. To perform the same type of opponent elbow control, you will need to quickly slide slightly outward, to the side of this stance, and then move in, shoving the lead elbow into his body.

Control and Counterattack

Once you have instigated initial elbow control, you must immediately unleash a secondary form of attack to assure your victory. This can be as simple as the previously illustrated Straight Punch to the face, or a Roundhouse Kick to the midsection.

The Advantages of Elbow Control

As you now understand, this type of opponent elbow control is one of the most effective methods of initial self-defense you can launch at the outset of a physical confrontation. With this style of preliminary self-defense, you maintain the ability to deliver the first strike and you are not faced with the necessity of attempting to block or deflect any of your opponent's offensive attacks. And by starting the defensive action, you will avoid being injured by one of your opponent's punches or kicks.

Common Mistakes of Elbow Control

The leading mistake in using elbow control as your primary technique for self-defense is not protecting yourself if your opponent recognizes your oncoming movement and rapidly redeploys his body and launches a secondary attack. For this reason, as is detailed in the Theory of Continuous Motion (page 31), you must always be ready to move out of the path of his attack and reformulate your defense.

Defending Against the Punching Attack

On open ground—do not try to block the enemy's way.

—S U N   T Z U

N ever encounter your opponent directly. By being evasive, he or she will not know what to expect, and thus cannot plan ahead in any attack upon you. What is seen is known; what is unseen is a mystery. Face your opponent and he will know who his adversary is. Try to stop him and he has the potential to overpower you with brute force. Stand aside, let your opponent pass; let him feel he has already won the battle. Then your defense and eventual victory will come as a surprise.

The punch is undoubtedly the most universally used offensive weapon in a street altercation. Most martial arts schools and self-defense courses teach various formal blocks to encounter an opponent's punch. This type of training is far too sterile, however, for the wild and random punches an attacker will throw at you on the street. To develop a truly effective punch defense, you must study the elements of all the punching techniques and then master the best method to countermand them.

Martial artists are traditionally trained to defend themselves against various punching attacks by using powerful blocking techniques. By blocking attacks forcefully, you may well stop an oncoming punch, but in doing so, you may also damage the blocking component of your own body—be it your hand, arm, or forearm. It has been proven time and time again in street confrontations and professional competitions alike, that by meeting force with force, bone to bone, the person who is deliberately blocking a very powerful offensive fighting technique will oftentimes damage the part of his own body he is using to block the punch. Therefore, to begin your mastery of punch defense methodology, the first thing you must discard is the concept that forceful blocking is a viable first line of defense against the street punch.

THE ART OF DEFLECTION

The instant question that arises is, "If I cannot block a punch, how can I defend myself?" There is a much more refined method of punch defense than that of the forceful block. That method is known as the art of deflection. Deflection is the primary tool of effective punch defense. It is your reaction to an opponent's forceful assault. You observe the pattern, be it linear or circular, of any attack your adversary is unleashing against you. Then, instead of forcefully encountering the attack, you simply move out of its path and guide the forceful energy away from your body by using your adversary's own momentum-driven aggressive power against himself.

The simplest application of effective opponent punch-deflection has you actually do nothing at all to intercept—or even touch—your adversary, once he has launched an aggressive attack at you! The art of deflection teaches you simply to move out of the path of an oncoming strike. For example, in the case of a Straight Punch, you would simply lean sideways, and it will miss you. Thus, the attempted strike did not harm you, as you neither received the impact of the hit nor have you forcefully intercepted it with a blocking technique. In addition, by doing nothing but moving out of the path of the attack, you have allowed your opponent's momentum to set him up for counterassault.

Moving out of the path of an oncoming punching attack will initially keep you free from injury, but avoidance is generally never enough to win in a confrontation. Your attacker may instantly launch a powerful secondary attack if you don't immediately dominate his movements. For this reason, the art of deflection teaches that it is imperative to take control over an attacker and guide his aggressive energy in a manner that will readily expose him to counterattack.

The art of deflection teaches that the time to launch self-defense countermeasures is the second your opponent's attack has been deflected. This is the fleeting moment when he is most vulnerable, as his balance is somewhat misaligned, and his mind is recalculating what move to make next. Therefore, this is your ideal opportunity to launch a counterattack.

DEFLECTING AND COUNTERATTACKING THE STRAIGHT PUNCH

Your attacker attempts to Straight Punch you. Initially, you side-step the punch, out of harm's way. Simultaneously, you perform an in-to-out forearm deflection against his outstretched punching arm. By sidestepping and deflecting the punch, you keep your opponent's energy moving forward, something that a forceful block will never achieve. In addition, you have kept his attacking arm held in check, so it cannot immediately launch a secondary attack at you—perhaps in the form of a Back Fist to your head. Once you have deflected the punch, and you hold his arm in check, you must instantly unleash a secondary counterattack. The simplest of these is a low Side Kick to his knee (see figure 20).

Using Your Opponent's Aggressive Energy

To take the art of deflection to the next level, you will want to use your attacker's aggressive energy to your own advantage. For example, in the case of the previously unleashed Straight Punch, you will witness that once his punch was deflected, the physical energy he instigated in unleashing it caused him to continue to move forward until he was virtually next to you, body-to-body. This happened because the aggressive energy of his Straight Punch was rerouted by your forearm deflection. Thus, he continued to move unintentionally forward in a linear pattern.

To further take advantage of his forward-driven energy and to unleash a powerful counterattack in the process of your punch deflection, all you need to do, once his punching arm has been rerouted, is to keep his energy moving by grabbing hold of his arm and pulling him in a downward pattern. As you do, drive a powerful Knee Strike into his midsection. (See figure 21 on pages 86 and 87.)

21C

Benefits of the Deflective Counterassault

From this style of opponent deflection you discover that not only has your adversary's attack missed you, but you deflected his punch, causing him to continue to move in the pattern of attack he instigated. Thus, it is his own energy that guides him forward as your knee powerfully impacts his midsection. The power of this counterstrike is, therefore, substantially increased as his own aggressive force helps drive him forward into your knee.

From this style of deflective defensive action, your adversary's attack is not only nullified, but you delivered a substantial first strike! Thus, you set the stage for your victory in the confrontation.

STRAIGHT   PUNCH   DEFLECTION —
THE   NEXT   STEP

No one technique is universally effective in all combat situations. This is also true in the case of defending against a very specific style of attack, such as the Straight Punch. For this reason, you will want to master a few applications of opponent deflection in order to be prepared for the slight variations that are present in each type of assault.

The Straight Punch Deflective Throw

As you begin to master the understanding of the art of deflection, you may wish to take its defensive applications to more exacting levels. This can readily be accomplished by integrating more advanced deflections and opponent control methods into your understanding. The moves are shown in figure 22 on pages 88–90.

For example, your opponent Straight Punches at you. You side-step the attack, as you circularly move your arms and deflect his punching

arm. You continue forward in the path of continuous motion and reach your deflecting hand over your opponent's punching arm, while your free arm moves in and keeps his arm in check. As you do so, you rapidly move your leg, which is closest to him, behind his rear leg. In

place, you instantly impact his face with your hand, powerfully sending him backward to the ground.

THE ROUNDHOUSE PUNCH

Random, wildly thrown, circular attacks are much more common in street altercations than the highly refined Straight Punch. These are ideally characterized by the wildly thrown Roundhouse Punch.

The Roundhouse Punch begins at shoulder level and is thrown first outward and is then guided in toward its target. The power of the Roundhouse Punch is developed from the momentum gained by its inward swing.

Due to the random and momentum-driven nature of the Roundhouse Punch, it is not easily retractable or readily refocused once it has been unleashed. Therefore, as an astute self-defense technician, you can take advantage of the relatively slow speed and obvious nature of this punch by rapidly stepping back out of its path. From this initial level of deflective self-defense, your attacker's own punching

23A

23B

23C

momentum will cause him to continue through with the force of his punch and easy self-defense measures can be unleashed, such as a Front Kick to his groin (see figure 23 on pages 91–93).

Deflection and Interception

The art of deflection teaches that you must never allow yourself to feel the full force of an adversary's attack, and you must take rapid and decisive action to ensure that you will emerge victorious from any confrontation. In certain applications, the first step in this process will be intercepting the attacking element of your opponent's body.

Perhaps your attacker Roundhouse Punches at you. Instead of simply stepping back out of its range, as you did with the previous example, you rapidly step in toward your attacker—inside his Roundhouse Punch. As you do, you intercept his punching arm with an in-to-out

forearm interception to his inner elbow region. With this, you have taken initial control over his aggressive body motion.

As this interception is certainly not enough to win in street combat, you must instantly take decisive measures to ensure your victory. To do this, while using his own aggressive energy, you will want to take hold of his shoulder with your intercepting hand, while you pivot on your feet, forcing him to continue in the pattern he has instigated with his assault. Continuing with the defined energy flow, you step behind his leg as you swing him out, and deliver a powerful Circle Hand Strike to his throat. This will cause him to be decisively sent back on the ground. (See figure 24 on pages 94 and 95.)

ROUNDHOUSE PUNCH INTERCEPTION — THE NEXT STEP

In the adrenal-filled moments of physical combat, your opponent may immediately launch a secondary Roundhouse Punching technique with his free arm, if his primary punch has been intercepted. As he does this, you must immediately take control over it, as you did with the first—with an in-to-out forearm interception. Once his attack has been nullified, and before he can attempt to wrestle you to the ground, you must deliver a powerful defensive strike, such as a knee to his groin. Once this has been accomplished, you must immediately follow up with additional self-defense to ensure your victory.

As you have him under control, you will not want to lose this superior positioning. Thus, your secondary line of defense will see you stepping behind him with one leg, and using it to sweep his legs out from under him as you send him to the ground. (See figure 25 on pages 97–99.)

You must never allow your opponent to have time to recover from the initial defense strikes you unleash. As he obviously means you harm, this will only allow him the opportunity to attack you once again. Therefore, as soon as you deliver any initial interception and striking technique, immediately follow it up with appropriate self-defense until your attacker is completely defeated. You can then leave with confidence that you will not be attacked from behind as you are exiting.

DEFLECTION DRILLS

Deflection drills allow you the opportunity to hone your skills by working with a training partner. Through practice, if you are ever accosted on the street, you will possess the inner knowledge of how to react to each type of punching attack and will not need to think about the method you should use as your best first line of self-defense.

Deflection Drill I

1. Face off with a training partner who is preferably wearing boxing gloves.

2. Locate yourself approximately 3 feet from one another (the average distance of a physical altercation).

3. Have him slowly throw a right-handed Straight Punch aimed at your head.

4. As this punch is extending, pivot slightly to the outside and deflect the punch with your left hand encountering his forearm (as was detailed in figure 21, on pages 86–87).

5. Return to your original position and allow him to perform the Straight Punch with his left hand as you deflect with your right.

6. Continue this process, allowing your training partner to increase the speed with each punch.

This drill will allow you to develop the ability to naturally, and without a thought, move out of the path and instantly deflect a Straight Punch.

Deflection Drill II

Once you become competent with Deflection Drill I, you must take Straight Punch deflection to the next level and apply counterdefensive measures to your deflection techniques. Without a counterstrike, you can deflect forever and your opponent will not cease his attack.

1. Deflect the Straight Punch attack as in Drill I.

2. Immediately upon your successful deflection, apply a counter-

defensive action. Try various techniques and see which is most efficient for you:

- a low Side Kick to the knee;
- a Knife Hand to the neck;
- a Back Fist to the face; or
- an Elbow Strike to the temples.

From this drill you will learn to instantly deflect and counterstrike any attacker.

Deflection Drill III

The Roundhouse Punch is a very common offensive tool for the untrained fighter. To develop the natural ability to effectively defend against this type of assault, face off with a training partner who is wearing boxing gloves.

1. Your partner directs a Roundhouse Punch at you with his left hand.

2. Step back; deflect it by slapping it downward with your right hand, impacting him to his wrist/forearm region.

3. Your training partner unleashes a secondary Roundhouse Punch with his right hand.

4. Step back; deflect it downward with your left hand.

5. As you increase your competency with Roundhouse Punch deflection, have your partner speed up and unleash one Roundhouse Punch after the next.

6. Continue to deflect each punch until you feel that it is time to counterstrike. Deliver a Straight Punch to his face.

CLOSE CONTACT DEFLECTION

In the previous deflection scenarios, you had the ability to move out of the path of your attacker's advance while applying deflection defense against his punches. This will not always be the case. In certain fighting situations you will be forced to encounter your opponent in very close quarters, and you will not have the ability to move out of the path of his attack.

Close contact self-defense does not mean that you must resort to traditional blocking techniques. You can still use deflection as your primary tool of defense. Your method of deflection simply must be altered.

During close contact fighting, your deflection is performed by using your hands and forearms to wipe away the punching attacks of your opponent.

Close Contact Deflection Drill

1. Place your back against a wall.

2. Bend your elbows to a 45-degree angle and place them at midbody level, approximately 6 inches in front of your torso.

3. Let your right forearm and hand swing up and down in front of your body, pivoting off your elbow like a windshield wiper.

4. When your arm returns to its first position, allow your left arm to move in a downward sweep in a similar fashion (see figure 26 on pages 103 and 104).

This deflective movement is not a stationary technique. You do not lock your arms at the 6-inch distance from your body, and keep them in place, no matter what. This close contact deflection is designed to

26A

26B

26C

26D

26E

move as your opponent moves. If your opponent punches slightly higher, your deflecting arm moves up to shoulder level. If he punches or kicks lower, your arms move to a lower position. Additionally, once the deflection of his attack has been actualized, you can grab hold of his arm and counterstrike as necessary.

It is also important to remember that the instant you move out of the path of your assailant's assault, you must follow up with a counterattack. Your attacker is most vulnerable at this point—his attack has missed and he has not had the time to prepare to launch a secondary assault. Thus, he is open for counterattack.

DEFLECTION AGAINST MULTIPLE OPPONENTS

In street encounters it is very common for an attacker's friends to join in on the assault against you. Your deflection defense against this type of attack must be very rapid and extremely debilitating.

When you are engaged in battle with multiple attackers, you must keep your movements fluid and continual. You should not engage a single attacker in battle. Instead, you must deflect, hit, and move through the various assailants.

For example, a group of attackers comes toward you and confrontation is imminent: strike the lead opponent with a powerful offensive technique, such as a low Side Kick to his knee or a penetrating Front Kick to his groin. Immediately, shove your way through the crowd of attackers. This will force them to realign their placement and turn to face you. In this moment of confusion, you can deliver a powerful offensive technique, such as the stepping Side Kick to another one of the attackers. Again, you must immediately move through or around them, reestablish your defensive placement, and attack before they have the ability to regroup.

In the multiple attacker scenario it is most important to avoid ending up on the ground! If you do, your chances of recovery are severely minimized. By continually moving through your opponents and deflecting any attack they attempt to launch at you while you counterattack, you can emerge victorious from this severe level of street confrontation.

PITFALLS OF DEFLECTION

It is essential to maintain your balance when you quickly step back and away from the path of an attack. You can lose your balance by hitting the curb or an unseen object, or simply trip over your own two feet. If you fall to the ground, your self-defense advantage will be substantially decreased. Additionally, you cannot hope to deflect the onslaught of an attacker's shoves, punches, or kicks forever. When you begin to master the understanding of deflection, you will realize how easy it is to defend yourself in this manner. From this, you may become overconfident and, at the outset of battle, you may begin to toy with your attacker—continually deflecting those advances. Sooner or later, if you do not counterstrike, an offensive advance will break through and hit you. The outcome of the confrontation may be defined by this assault. Therefore, you must always rapidly counterattack and halt the onslaught as soon as possible.

Defending Against the Grabbing Attack

Yield and overcome.
Bend and be straight.
Be empty and become full.
Tire and become revitalized.
—LAO TZU

The modern world has programmed us into believing that more is better, bigger is better, strength is better, power is better, and control is better. But if we look at life from a different perspective, we come to realize that control over another individual means that we must continually take care of that person, power means that we must constantly fight to maintain it, strength must be perpetually exercised, bigger means that we must maintain our stature, and more means we must always find a way to pay for methods to obtain it.

If we desire nothing, have nothing to prove, and no one to prove it to, we are free, and then all power, strength, and desire is ours—because we already possess all that we need.

THE GRAB

Grabbing is oftentimes an assailant's first method of attack. Though a grab is not as debilitating as a powerful punch or a kick, a grabbing attack can escalate to a point where you may become severely injured. For this reason, if you are grabbed, learn how to immediately free yourself.

Recklessly attempting to free yourself from a grabbing attack by pulling and jerking serves little purpose. As your attacker has no doubt taken a firm hold on you, the strength of his grasp will only increase if you randomly attempt to pull free. Additionally, as he has already established a superior offensive position, if you aimlessly struggle, he may simply change his mode of attack and begin to deliver severe blows. Therefore, recklessly fighting to free yourself from a body grab is never your best self-defense.

Two Primary Rules for the Grabbing Attack

To master the appropriate methods to defend against the various types of grabbing assaults, there are two primary rules to follow:

1. You must immediately launch into self-defense the moment you are grabbed.

2. No defensive movement should ever be made unless it will have a substantially debilitating effect upon your grabbing attacker.

Defensive Applications for the Grab

Once you have been forcefully grabbed by an attacker, you must immediately shift your mind and body into precise defensive action. Allowing any time to elapse will allow your opponent to strengthen his hold on you. As seconds progress, his ability to dominate the confrontation will increase and yours will decrease. Therefore, the moment you are grabbed, immediately position yourself by planting your feet firmly on the ground and striking your opponent in the most debilitating location you can easily access. This first strike action will not only loosen any hold he has on you, but will stun him to the degree where you can follow through with additional self-defense as necessary.

THE REAR GRAB

Being grabbed from the rear is often the first offensive action an attacker will launch. As you generally do not possess the ability to see this attack coming, it can prove to be very dangerous if you do not immediately deal with the assault.

Many people, when grabbed from behind, immediately attempt to turn and face their attacker. Though this is the natural instinct, attempting to turn is only an applicable defense when you can deliver a powerful first strike, such as a rear Elbow Strike to the temple, in the process. If your attacker already substantiated his grasp upon you, recklessly attempting to turn not only wastes your own energy but leaves you open to further striking assaults, as well.

To study the rear grab more precisely we must view the various forms it takes and learn how best defend against each type of rear grab attack.

THE ONE-HANDED REAR GRAB

An attacker has grabbed you by the rear shoulder and is pulling you back with one hand. Instead of allowing his grasp to control your motion and possibly send you backward to the ground, immediately realign your footing by stepping back toward him. By doing this, even though he still has you in his grasp, you will at least have substantiated

competent footing. (See figure 27.)

Immediately upon the realignment of your footing, move into an offensive posture and strike your opponent. As he has pulled you back toward him, this initial strike may well be actualized by pivoting toward him, on your now stable rear leg, and you can strike him with a rear elbow to his face or temple.

By allowing the force of your attacker's backward pull to define the type of defensive action you take, you not only gain speed in your counterattack, but you gain additional momentum-driven strike power, as well. This is due to the fact that your attacker has already used his own energy to pull you backward. Thus, by allowing his pulling energy to move you

in toward him, all you have to do is strike him with your most easily available weapon, which is your elbow. Thus, you use little of your own energy in your defense.

Once you have made this initial strike, you must follow forward with the theory of continual motion by continuing through with your striking pivot. You can substantiate your control over the confrontation by initially holding your attacker's grabbing hand in place on your shoulder. Then you reach your striking arm circularly under and then over his arm, placing your hand at his shoulder joint. You rapidly move your grasping hand onto the inner region of his arm. Now, by powerfully coming down on his shoulder joint, while shoving his grabbing arm back toward his spine, his shoulder will be locked, leaving you in control of the confrontation. (See figure 27e.)

THE TWO-HANDED
REAR SHOULDER GRAB

In certain defensive scenarios, the energy your assailant expends in his grabbing attack is all you need to place yourself in the appropriate defensive posture. For example, if your opponent has taken hold of you and is pulling you backward at your shoulder level with both hands, you can easily move backward with the energy of his attack—waiting for the appropriate moment of action.

To defend yourself in this waiting fashion, you must first and foremost remain conscious of your footing. (See figure 28, pages 113–115.) Then, by waiting for the moment when his backward pulling force has ceased, you rapidly step one of your feet back, behind the other, substantiating your position. You then powerfully drive a fist into your

opponent's groin. Once this strike has made impact, you must immediately follow through by turning around to face your attacker to deliver additional frontal strikes as necessary, such as a Palm Strike to his nose.

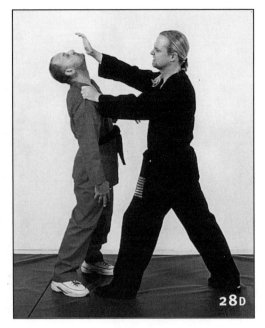

THE SIDE GRAB

If an attacker grabs you by your upper shirt or coat sleeve from the side, your defense is much more easily applied than in the case of your being grabbed from behind. The moment he has taken hold, bring the arm closest to him circularly up, over, and then under his grabbing arm. Powerfully bring your arm up under his central upper arm region. This will initially lock his grabbing arm in place. If you continue through with your power, it can even break his shoulder. In either case, you can complete your self-defense by delivering a Knife Hand strike to his throat—which will immediately disable him. (See figure 29 on pages 116–118.)

THE BODY GRAB

Not all grabs are as easily defended against as the previously described cases. At times, an attacking opponent may forcefully take hold of your entire body from the rear, locking your arms down to your side. With this move, your arms will not be available to be used as defensive tools.

Your first method of defense will be to immediately strike your opponent with any bodily weapon you can use. For example, you can stomp on the top of his foot, powerfully and repeatedly, with the heel of your foot. You can forcefully swing your leg out to gain momentum and then drive your rear heel into his shin or knee. Or, you can then lean your head forward at neck level and vigorously smash the back of your head into his nose region. These striking techniques should be performed contin-

ually until they have the effect of loosening, if not completely disengaging, the attacker's hold on your body. (See figure 30 on pages 120–122.)

You must remain very conscious when these strikes are being delivered. You must feel for the moment when he loosens his grasp on you, as this is the time to break away. When his hold is diminishing, form your hands in Knife Hands, as this will tense the muscles of your entire arm. As you pull free, do so in a very decisive manner, with your arms traveling in a linear path away from your body. This is the most efficient way to completely disengage his hold.

As is the case with all grabbing defense, never attempt to randomly pull yourself free. This only unnecessarily expends your energy and generally proves to be less than effective.

Once you are free, immediately begin to deliver defensive strikes. This can be accomplished by initially pivoting and delivering an elbow

strike to his midsection or head. Follow through with additional powerful strike techniques, such as a Front Kick to his groin. In this way, he will not be able to come back at you with additional offensive maneuvers.

THE STANDING REAR-CHOKE HOLD

One of the most serious types of rear grabs takes place when you are attacked with a Standing Rear-Choke Hold. Not only is the force of this grab very dangerous to your trachea, but with the Standing Rear-Choke Hold, your spine is arched backward, leaving you in an injury-prone position. Therefore, you must disengage a Rear-Choke Hold immediately, before it has the ability to render you unconscious from lack of oxygen, or critically injure your spine.

The first step in your defense against the Standing Rear-Choke Hold is to instantly strike your attacker. This can be most quickly accomplished by delivering several fist strikes to your attacker's groin. Once his hold has loosened, by pivoting on your rear foot, your can unleash multiple Elbow Strikes to his ribs and head.

By this time, your attacker's hold will be fully released. You can rapidly leave the location, or you can continue your counterattacking defense upon him so he will not be able to recover by pivoting to face him and delivering a Palm Strike to his nose. (See figure 31 on pages 123 and 124.)

THE KNEELING REAR-CHOKE HOLD

Another potentially deadly choke hold is the Kneeling Rear-Choke Hold (figure 32). This is where your attacker jumps on you from behind, attacking with the weight of his body, ultimately driving you down to your knees, while he maintains a head-locking choke hold on you.

The moment you find yourself engulfed in this type of attack, you must strike. The best first strike location is to reach behind your attacker's back and deliver a rear Knife Hand to his groin. This will loosen his hold on you. Immediately after your strike, you should reach your same striking hand up and over his choking arms, and place your middle finger horizontally under his nose. By powerfully shoving up

and back on this nerve center, his grasp will be released and he will be sent to the floor, on his back, where additional self-defense can be unleashed as necessary. (See figure 32 on pages 125–127.)

FRONTAL-CHOKE HOLD I

Whereas ill-intentioned criminals generally advance from the rear, barroom fighters will often come at you from the front. This is due to the fact that they are oftentimes intoxicated and are angered for some nonspecific reason. If punches are not being thrown, the Frontal-Choke Hold is your adversary's most probable form of grabbing assault.

You are being held in a Frontal-Choke Hold. Bring one of your arms up and over your attacker's arms. Make your hand in the Knife Hand formation. Start as high as possible, at a 45-degree angle, and bring your arm in a continuous pattern down across his choking arms as you pivot your spine in the direction of your movement. His grasp will be released. Immediately come back with a Rear Elbow Strike to his face. (See figure 33.)

FRONTAL-CHOKE HOLD II

An attacker has shoved you against a wall while performing a two-handed Frontal-Choke Hold to your neck. His body is, no doubt, a foot or so away from yours, bridged by his extended arms. Thereby, he has left his jaw highly exposed. By delivering a powerful uppercut punch to his jaw, his choke hold will be instantly released.

Now that his grasp on your neck has been dislodged, allow your environment to lead you to your secondary level of self-defense. Since your back is against a wall, use this location to your advantage. You can easily side-step your attacker and, by reaching behind his arms and taking control of one of his shoulders, shove his face powerfully into the wall. This will end the confrontation in your favor. (See figure 34 on pages 130–131.)

34A

THE KICK GRAB

Grabbing attacks don't always take the form of unsuspected body-grabs. Oftentimes, they are unleashed in the midst of a physical altercation. For example, if you have launched a Front Kick toward an opponent, one of the most common occurrences is that he will immediately grab hold of your kicking leg just after striking contact has been made. This takes no training; it's simply a reflex action. Therefore, even though you may have made the first strike, your superior advantage will quickly diminish if you don't instantly free yourself from his grasp. The common mistake that many novice self-defense technicians make, when the kicking leg has been grabbed, is to recklessly attempt to pull it free. And then the opponent will have the opportunity to wrestle you to the ground, which is to no one's advantage.

If your kicking leg has been grabbed, instead of struggling to free yourself, grab him somewhere to *your* advantage. If your leg is being held, this means you are in close proximity to him. Allow his hold on your leg to define your motion, and immediately jump in toward him, powerfully punching him in his face. As you rapidly move in toward him, put your weight and the forward momentum of your body onto your captured leg. This force, in association with your punch, will immediately cause him to let go of your leg. You will then be free to follow through with additional self-defense, as necessary. (See figure 35 on pages 132 and 133.)

The grabbing attack can be unleashed from any number of locations. As you now understand, you don't have to fear it. Instead, you simply apply your first strike advantage and then use your attacker's own aggressive energy against himself to defeat him, so you can emerge victorious from the confrontation.

MAKING MISTAKES
IF YOU ARE GRABBED

The largest problem that people encounter when accosted by a grabbing attacker is that they are so startled from the initial grab that they forget to act immediately. This allows the attacker to substantiate his hold.

This reaction—being startled—can be somewhat curtailed by partner practice. But, as you are expecting an attack in partner practice, you are emotionally ready, and it is the lack of readiness that causes individuals to be defeated by grabbing attacks.

In the case of a street grab, you must react immediately. Train your mind to be on full alert, and think of what you will do to countermand each type of grabbing attack as you walk through new locations. By doing this, you will remain ready, and you won't be surprised.

From an enlightenment point of view, you can keep in mind that you are not the center of the universe. Most people who are attacked are thinking of themselves—their lives, their feelings, their world. There are other people in the world, too, and those other people may have different plans. If we allow ourselves to think of a larger universe, knowing we are only part of a great "whole," we won't be surprised when we walk in strange neighborhoods.

Grappling and Ground Fighting

In the science of martial arts, your state of mind should constantly remain

undistracted. Center your mind: from this, there will be no imbalance.

Allow there to be no perceivable difference between your ordinary and your

martial arts' mind. It is imperative to master the principles of the art of

war and to maintain an unmovable mind, even in the heart of battle.

—MIYAMOTO MUSASHI

T he techniques of warfare are not only designed to be practiced in a martial arts studio or in the heat of battle: they can become the essence of your being. The martial arts, though based in warfare, are not warfare. They form a particular technique that allows the practitioner to view life from a more profound place. This is due to the fact that the practitioner has, through continued practice, come to understand the nature of human movement and how the energy of life interacts with the energy of nature and with the energy of the universe. So if you think martial arts is only about fighting— think again.

HAND-TO-HAND COMBAT

An enraged attacker grabs you by the shoulder. At the moment you turn to encounter him, he flings his body at yours and the two of you land on the ground, with him on top. You find yourself looking up at his fists powerfully punching down at you.

Ending up in this type of ground-fighting situation is no doubt one of the most common occurrences that can happen to even the best trained self-defense strategist. This can happen because, on the street, your attacker will no doubt strike at you with every available weapon he has, in order that he may emerge victorious in the confrontation. Oftentimes the weight of his body is his first line of offense.

The leading mistake most people make when they find themselves on the bottom end of a ground-fighting encounter is to attempt to haphazardly punch back up at their attacker, who has the upper position. This type of defense is not only a waste of energy, but it serves little purpose, as the attacker will maintain the superior position and continue his assault with more powerful punches than we are able to deliver from our current location on the ground.

The second common mistake people make, once they find themselves on the ground, is to recklessly attempt to wiggle their way out from underneath the attacker. This type of misdirected grappling also proves to be a pointless waste of energy, as we are doing nothing to scientifically free ourselves.

GROUND-FIGHTING BASICS

If you find yourself on the bottom end of a ground-fighting confrontation, your attacker's punches need only travel in a downward path. The attacker has additional gravitational force and momentum on his side. This type of punching attack must be halted immediately or you can very easily be knocked out or severely injured if the assault continues unabated.

If you find yourself looking up at your attacker, don't waste time trying to block his punches. This is a fruitless exercise at best, and the most you can hope to accomplish is to shield your face from his oncoming attack with your arms. And if you do this, you keep your arms from applying any appropriate self-defense.

The time to launch ground-fighting defense is the moment you find yourself on the floor. You must first stop any type of forceful attack your opponent may be launching at your head, and then immediately follow up with a competent counterattack. The most efficient way to accomplish this is to encounter his attack in a way that will not only stop his assault on you but will also give you a defensive position from where you can get him off you so you can continue forward with additional self-defense as necessary.

Four Rules for Ground Fighting

1. Never attempt to defend yourself from a position of inadequacy.

2. Use your attacker's own random, undirected energy to place yourself in a superior combat position.

3. Anticipate your attacker's motions and use his own energy against himself.

4. Never block, when you can gain control of a grappling confrontation by launching your own attack.

GROUND FIGHT PUNCHING DEFENSE I

In a ground level punching assault, your attacker will generally hold you to the ground with one arm, known as his "base arm," as he punches at you with his "striking arm." Halting the attack and getting him off you is initialized by first striking your attacker at a vital point. (See figure 36 on pages 140–143.)

This first defensive strike may well be best applied by hitting him at the base of his nose with a Palm Strike. To substantiate the power of this strike, you want to hold his base arm in place by grabbing hold of it with your nonstriking hand. In this way, your opponent will not be readily able to lean back out of the path of your counterattack.

This initial defensive strike, though not necessarily completely debilitating, will momentarily halt your opponent's assault, providing you with an opportunity to remove him from his upper position. This can be done by leaving your striking hand in place as you simultaneously pull down on his base arm, which you already have a hold upon, as you push up and over with your striking hand, which is lodged beneath his nose. With this, you send him over himself, landing with his back on the ground. Thus, you will have gained the upper position strike advantage, where you can deliver appropriate powerful striking techniques to his face (see figure 36e).

GROUND-FIGHT
PUNCHING DEFENSE II

A second very suitable option when you are on the bottom of a ground-fighting encounter is to strike at your attacker's base arm elbow from the outside before he has a chance to punch at you. This is most effectively accomplished by grabbing onto the upper portion of the hand of his base arm where it encounters your body. This will effectively lock it in place. Then, with your other hand, powerfully Palm Strike to the outer area of his elbow. By maintaining control over his hand while impacting his outer elbow, you will force him, face first, to travel downward toward the ground. Once he is in this position, you can easily slide from under him and deliver a powerful strike to the back of his head. (See figure 37 on pages 143–145.)

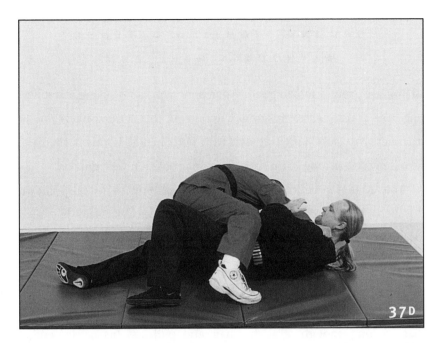

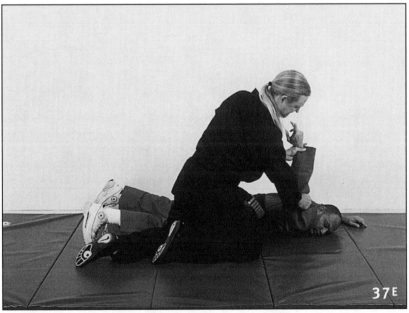

GROUND-FIGHTING DEFENSE
WITHOUT A BASE ARM

If you are ground fighting, and your opponent is not using a stabilizing base arm to isolate his attack upon you, this is most likely due to the fact that he is punching you with both hands. If this is the case, you'll need to remove him from his upper position very quickly!

Your first step will be to deliver an initial blow to a vital point on his body to cause him to interrupt his attack. Once this has been accomplished, rapidly reach up, with your nonstriking hand, impact his chin and immediately arch his neck to one side by powerfully pushing it away from you. As you do so, bring your other hand up and take hold of the back of his head, pulling it down toward you. If his hair is long enough, grab his hair and pull, as this causes added

38A

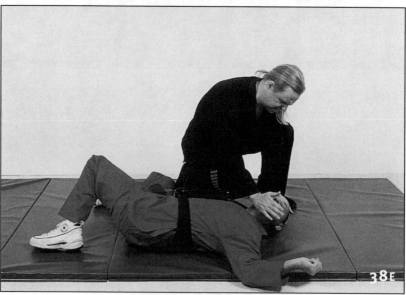

control and pain. This two-handed technique will effectively lock his neck. He is easily directed off if you continue through with the neck-twisting motion. Once he has been removed, and you have the upper position, you can perform additional counterstriking techniques as necessary. (See figure 38 on pages 146–148.)

GROUND LEVEL
CHOKE HOLD

The ground level choke hold is a common type of ground fighting attack. Attempting to wrestle loose the hands of the attacker is never your best form of self-defense, as you may lose consciousness, due to lack of air, before you are free. Therefore, to effectively defend against a ground-level choking attack, you must rapidly take control of the confrontation. (See figure 39 on pages 149–151.)

If you find yourself being held in a ground level choke hold and your attacker's arms are outstretched, you can dislodge his hold by bringing both your arms up over the top of his arms while you simultaneously deliver Knife Hand strikes to his inner elbows. This will cause his arms to bend inward and he will loosen his grasp. Once you have achieved this, you must immediately get him off your body. To

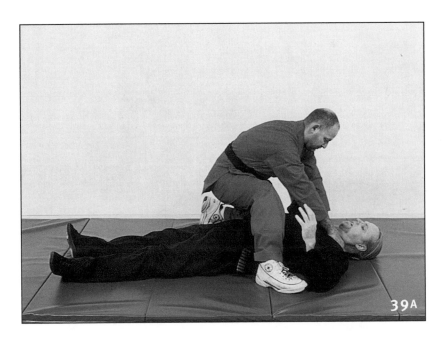

39A

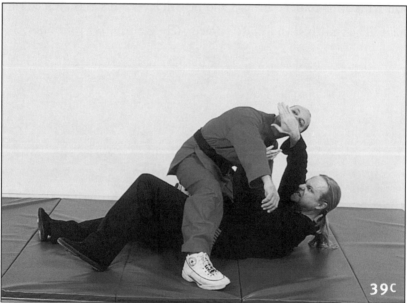

achieve this, strike and lock a Knife Hand under the base of his nose, as you powerfully push back. With your right hand, remove his left

arm from on top of you, as you slide out from under him. Come up to
your knees, release your hand, and powerfully punch his face.

TACKLE DEFENSE 1

The tackle take-down has been very effective in removing an opponent from his feet in fighting competitions like the "Ultimate Fighting Championship." The savvy no-holds-barred fighter will generally launch himself from one knee as he attempts a tackle take-down. In this way, he hopes to maintain his ability to return to a standing position if the technique doesn't prove effective. This style of tackle leaves his head in a prone, upward position, making it a target in your defense strategy.

As the opponent launches himself at you, move in. This will, first of all, intercept the forward driving tackling momentum. Thus, his force will be nullified. As you step in, drive your rear knee powerfully forward and into the face of your attacker. This technique can be aided by grabbing hold of the back of his head. The combination of powerfully

40A

kneeing him in the face, with the addition of shoving his face into your knee, will instantly debilitate him (see figure 40).

TACKLE DEFENSE II

In some cases, you will not have the foresight to defend yourself before your attacker has substantiated his tackling offensive at you. In these cases, you must defend yourself as you travel toward the ground. When an attacker is jumping you, the first thing to do is deflect one of his arms slightly to one side of your body, as you are traveling down toward the ground. (See figure 41 on pages 154–156.) Though it may be too late to save yourself from the actual ground fight, by accomplishing this deflection you will both land on the ground side by side, and your attacker will not have the advantage of being on top of you. Furthermore, if you keep your deflecting hand in place, near his

shoulder level, once you hit the ground, you can maintain substantial control over him. This control is accomplished by maintaining pressure on the back of his shoulder, and holding him face down toward the ground.

Once your opponent's initial attack has been nullified and he is held in place, you can rapidly get up on your knees and unleash a devastating punch to the back of his head (see figure 41e).

KICKED ON THE GROUND

One of the worst case scenarios to find yourself in is to be on the ground with your attacker kicking you. Though this is a dangerous position to be in, there is an effective method to countermand it (shown in figure 42 on pages 157–158).

Your attacker kicks you as you look up at him from the ground. This kick will traditionally be performed in Front Kick styling. Before he has the opportunity to truly injure you, extend the arm closest to his kicking leg, parallel to the ground. Encounter his kicking leg with your forearm at shin level. Immediately, once his kick has been intercepted, reach your free hand behind his ankle and grab hold of it. Raise your body off the ground at waist level as you simultaneously pull up on his ankle and push back on his shin. Your attacker will be sent to the ground, where additional counterattacks may be launched as necessary.

KICKING FROM THE GROUND

If you find yourself on the ground but you have not yet been attacked, you must immediately take defensive action before the confrontation becomes critical. An attacker is moving in on you. Roll to your side.

43

Place both hands firmly on the ground to substantiate your action. Lift the upper part of your body off the ground. Recoil your leg and kick, in Side Kick fashion, to his knee or midsection. Immediately get up (see figure 43 on page 159).

Ground fighting does not have to be a complicated fighting experience. The key to effective grappling is to never allow your opponent to remain in a superior combative position to you. Instead, take control of the encounter by making every movement you make count, and by leaving nothing to random motion. You can achieve this by taking advantage of the elements of your opponent's body and using them to your own advantage.

Ending up on the ground is never to your advantage. It is the worst case scenario for any fighting situation. To this end, you must strive to keep yourself standing in all physical altercations.

Defending Against Weapons

Weapons are inauspicious implements.
They are contrary to virtue.
—WEI LIAO-TZU

A good weapon is an instrument of fear.
All creatures have distaste for them.
The man of Tao never touches a weapon.
—LAO TZU

The warriors who used weapons in ancient times did not use them to
expand their kingdoms or gain more wealth, they only used weapons
for the survival of their kingdoms.
—HUAINANZI

All weapons which are designed to kill are inauspicious and must
never be used except in a case of extreme urgency.
—YAGYU MUNENORI

Virtually any physical object can be used as a weapon. There is a vast difference, however, between the motivation of utilizing an object to defend your honor or your life, and those intentionally used by an individual who desires only to overpower others. In many forms of martial arts, weapons once used in ancient times as implements of war are now used to train the body and eye coordination of the practitioner. Thus, this once violent object has evolved and become an instrument of refinement.

In all cases, the use of a weapon against another human being is a personal choice. When encountering a weapon-wielding opponent in battle, defeat him as quickly as possible—for if you do not, his low level of human interactive consciousness may allow him to hurt or kill you. Use your keenly focused mind and precise body movements as the tool to overpower his weapon.

- Your body is a weapon if you see it as a weapon.
- Your body is an instrument of truth and light if you see it as an instrument of truth and light.
- Your body—your choice. Live.

With the growing proliferation of violent crimes, and the use of weapons directly linked to these crimes, you must learn how to effectively defend against the various types of weapon assaults. The key element of weapon self-defense is to discard any technique that is too elaborate to be truly effective on the street. Oftentimes in martial arts and self-defense classes, weapon defenses are taught that are very intriguing to witness, but they possess no effectiveness when used against a weapon attack that takes place at the hands of a violent adversary on the street.

THE GUN

Guns are the most dangerous of all weapons. If your attacker possesses a gun, is willing to use it, and is at any distance from you, the best thing you can do is run. For the speed a bullet travels and the likelihood of it having the ability to fatally injure you is too great a risk to ever take the chance of moving toward a gun-wielding opponent and attempting to take the weapon away. When an attacker possesses a gun and is in close proximity to your body, however, there are certain self-defense techniques that can be effectively used to deflect its presence and defeat the attacker.

THE FRONTAL GUN ASSAULT

The simplest way to defend against a gun, in a frontal attack, is to rapidly deflect the gun-holding arm of the opponent outward, with an in-to-out forearm deflection, and then quickly Palm Strike the attacker under the base of his nose. By defending against the gun in this fashion, even if the trigger is pulled, with any luck your deflection will be rapid enough to have the bullet fly off into the air, hurting no one. (See figure 44 on pages 163 and 164.)

44A

R E A R   G U N   A T T A C K

If an assailant has accosted you from behind, it is common that he or she will announce the presence of a pistol by placing its barrel against your back. The moment you feel its presence is the time to take action! Immediately spin around, deflecting the weapon outward to a range where it cannot shoot you, and instantly Palm Strike your assailant under his nose. (See figure 45 on page 165.)

T H E   K N I F E

The knife has long been documented as a common assault oriented weapon. Virtually every self-defense system teaches methods to rapidly move in and catch the arm of the attacker who possesses a knife. Attempting to catch a knife is never effective for three reasons:

1. The attacker's arm has the potential to move too fast for you to be sure that you will be able to reach in and catch his knife-holding hand before he has a chance to realign his blade and cut your incoming hand.

2. Don't believe that the avid street fighter doesn't have the ability to see your hands moving toward him to catch his knife-holding arm. If you attempt to grab his arm, all he has to do is move slightly backward or to the side and, since you have rushed in on him, you will have left yourself prone to an easy stabbing attack from his knife.

3. By attempting to catch your attacker's knife-holding arm, you believe that when and if you can accomplish this, he will remain in one position, allowing you to control him and perform whatever type of self-defense technique you have planned. No, he will not! Inevitably, he will simply shift the knife in his hand and cut you.

You now understand that attempting to grab the knife-holding arm of an attacker is not a viable option. There are, however, a few highly refined methods to defend against the onslaught of a knife attack.

KNIFE-FIGHTING OFFENSIVE

The moment you are accosted by a knife-holding attacker you must take immediate action. If he has just positioned himself in front of you, and is either attempting to prepare his knife for combat, or is locating his knife to threaten you, this is the moment you must move in with a rapid offensive, such as a penetrating Front Kick to his groin.

As your attacker has not substantiated his hold on the knife, it will not be easy for him to redirect it and point it toward your kicking leg.

Additionally, he will not be expecting a counterassault so early in the confrontation. Thus, this is the prime time for you to unleash an attack. (See figure 46.)

The Wrapped Arm

If you must launch in at your knife-holding opponent after his knife is firmly grasped, the age-old method of wrapping a coat or sweater around your arm and hand is somewhat effective. By doing this, the knife will have difficulty penetrating the material. Thus, you can fake an inward advance at your opponent with your protected arm; then, while his knife is attempting to slash at this arm, you can begin to deliver debilitating blows such as low Side Kicks to his knee. (See figure 47.)

47A

KNIFE-FIGHTING DEFENSE

Defeating a knife-wielding attacker with a powerful offensive technique is the ideal circumstance. It is, however, not always possible. For this reason, you must learn to successfully defend against a knife attack once the blade is in motion.

One of the key things to watch for, whenever an attacker has accosted you with a knife, is his shoulder movement. He will generally move the shoulder, just a bit, before he actually sends the knife forward. This shoulder movement takes place either because he uses this motion to recoil his knife backward before he launches it inward, or he uses it to realign himself to better frame his path of attack. In either case, movement in his shoulder is the clue that a knife fight is imminent. Once you observe this shoulder motion, this is your time to prepare for the oncoming blade.

KNIFE DEFLECTION

Deflection is the key defensive element to remember when you encounter a knife attack. No matter what form of counterattack you choose to launch once the oncoming blade has been nullified, it must first be deflected before any further maneuvering can successfully be accomplished.

The Low Level Slash

The best form of deflection is to avoid the attacking blade. Thus, when defending against the low level slash, your first course of appropriate self-defense would be to rapidly move back out of the path of the slash. Once it passes you, instantly move in to take control over your attacker's elbow by shoving it tightly into his body. Then deliver a powerful counterstrike, such as a Knee Strike to his side. You would then follow

the theory of continual motion by locking his knife-holding arm tightly into his body as you spin him around and throw him to the ground over your extended leg. (See figure 48 on pages 171–173.)

48C

48D

48E

48F

INTERCEPTING

THE KNIFE ATTACK

Deflection of a knife-wielding attacker is not always possible. You must be the instigator here; you must intercept his knife-holding arm.

The Head Level Slash

An attacker attempts to launch a head level, circular slashing knife assault. You instantaneously step in and stop the knife's progress by performing a Knife Hand, In-to-Out cross-arm interception to his inner forearm region, as you did with the Roundhouse Punch. This technique should be performed as close to the attack's point of origin as possible. This will keep the knife assault from possessing momentum. Once this circular knife assault has been stopped, you must leave your intercepting arm in place and take hold of him at shoulder level to ensure your momentary control of his actions.

Once you have encountered the knife-holding arm, don't think that you have more than a second to successfully defend yourself before your opponent simply realigns the blade and cuts you. Your first defense must be a powerful Palm Strike under the base of his nose. At this point, as your opponent's arm is in check, and you have delivered a powerful first strike, you can send him to the ground by arching his knife-holding arm back in an unnatural pattern, as you pivot your body, directing him to the ground. (See figure 49 on pages 175–177.)

49F

49G

THE FORWARD

STABBING ASSAULT

The assailant who possesses a knife oftentimes will attempt to stab you with it. Whether or not he moves it from side to side in an effort to confuse you, as is common in street fights, is irrelevant, for sooner or later its blade will be launched in your direction.

Knife Stab—Outside Deflection

A knife is stabbed in your direction. You sidestep the attack, to the outside of the stab. You deflect the knife's stabbing action by performing a low level Knife Hand strike to the outside forearm of your attacker, as his arm is extended. Once this deflection is achieved, you must immediately take control over his arm. This is accomplished by pivoting your Knife Hand over and grabbing his forearm. As his knife is held in check, even if only for a moment, you follow through by delivering a Knife Hand across his throat. This will powerfully send him to the ground. (See figure 50 on pages 179–180.)

Knife-Fighting Warnings

In all knife deflection techniques it is imperative that you avoid grabbing your attacker's hand or arm in such a manner that it will allow him to come back and easily cut you. Don't lock yourself in a deflection technique so tightly that you can't quickly move out of it and away from your attacker.

THE CLUB

Pipes, chains, and clubs are some of the most commonly used weapons on the street. This is due to the fact that they are readily available. Though these weapons differ slightly in their design, you use similar techniques to defend against them. Therefore, the methods for this level of self-defense will be categorized under one heading.

CLUB DEFLECTION

From a self-defense standpoint, deflection of the club is easier to do than protecting yourself from a knife. This weapon cannot realign and cut you. Thus, your self-defense strategy is eased considerably.

Side-to-Side Club Deflection

A club is launched in a side-to-side assault on you. Step back out of the path of its attack, allowing the force created by the weapon's swing to

51A

carry the arm of your attacker through with its momentum. Counterstrike with a powerful stepping Side Kick to the opponent's body. (See figure 51 on pages 181–182.)

Overhead Club Deflection

As is the case with all aggressive weapon assaults, initially moving out of the path of the attack is most advantageous. For example, in the case of the overhead club assault, which is about to be swung downward—targeted at your cranium—your first line of defense will be to sidestep the attack. You then immediately place a hand to his club-wielding arm. This will hold it in check as you unleash additional self-defense. You immediately step in behind his leg as you simultaneously deliver a Knife Hand strike to his throat. This will send him over your leg and onto the ground. (See figure 52 on pages 183–186.)

52A

BLOCKING THE CLUB

At times it may be necessary to directly block the oncoming strike of a club. Due to the awkwardness of this weapon, this is generally accomplished by simply intercepting your attacker in midstrike position.

The most appropriate time to block a club strike is as close to its point of inception as possible. By intercepting the attack at this point, the striking arm of your attacker has not had the time to develop much velocity, and you will not be injured from the block.

Blocks against the club should be focused at mid-forearm level. At this location, not only is your attacker most susceptible to an effective block, but by blocking forearm-to-forearm you have a certain amount

53A

of range of movement and compensation if your assailant moves his technique slightly.

Interception

The downward club swing is in motion. With your arm parallel to the ground, you intercept the movement of your attacker. The moment his club strike has been intercepted, take the middle finger of your free hand and shove it into the inner elbow joint of his club-wielding arm. Use it as a wedge, as you shove his arm back over itself. Pivot your rear leg behind yourself, as you direct him to the ground. Additionally, striking self-defense can be used as necessary. (See figure 53 on pages 186–189.)

53B

53E

Cautions for Weapon Defense

Fighting against any weapon in a street confrontation is never a good situation. If you can leave the altercation, you should. If you can't, you must defend yourself with no regard for your attacker. Too many people initially defend themselves, but do not disable their assailants—only to find the assailant immediately comes back at them! If you are injured in a weapon assault, your further defense is virtually impossible. You have one shot; therefore, you must defend yourself to your utmost.

Training at Home

Chien killed Kuan. Ling-po and Chou killed Pi-kan. The victims were
very virtuous men. They lived their life attempting to give solace to people.
From these actions of goodness, the rulers became aware of their presence
and had them put to death. Why? Because they sought fame
for their actions of goodness.

—CHAUNG TZU

Do what you are going to do—that's life. When you believe
that your actions are good, not only is any virtue lost in ego-
tism, but you bring attention to yourself, negating the purity
of what you have accomplished. Life involves personal encounters.
From interaction, your intentions become obvious.

Be silent: then you, your mind, and your ideologies are pure because
they are not seen, judged, or commented upon. You do what you do,
and that's that. If your actions are witnessed, they can be counter-
manded.

HOMEWORK

Students who study at home often excel in the classroom. It is also true
that self-defense technicians who mentally think about the techniques
they have learned, and who practice them physically, become the most
competent practitioners. With this in mind, we must set about to

develop a practice schedule that will aid us in becoming more competent self-defense strategists.

A common form of home practice involves what has come to be known as shadow boxing. This involves randomly punching or kicking at imaginary targets in the air. This can be an effective way of warming up and getting our cardiovascular systems working. When done incorrectly, however, there are several less than desirable results attached to this form of practice. People can damage the body doing this.

SHADOW BOXING

Punching at imaginary targets loosens the upper body and, even when used in an uncontrolled manner, can exercise shoulder and arm muscles. This undirected punching, however, should not give you the impression that you are actually developing focus with your punching techniques. Quite the contrary, in fact. As you are punching haphazardly into the air you may believe you are directing your fists where you want them to go, but you have no actual way of measuring the effective strike point of your attack, or whether or not you actually made contact with the target you had in mind.

Powerfully punching toward a mirror is another method many budding self-defense technicians employ at home with the hopes of honing their punching skills. Though you can develop more precisely styled hand-strike techniques by watching your punch from start to finish in a mirror, again, beyond this you have no actual measure of whether or not you have actually hit your desired target.

Certainly, most of us believe we can direct our fists and make impact with our chosen target. In many cases, this is, no doubt, the truth, if our target is stationary. But, how many times in a physical confrontation does your opponent remain stagnant and allow you to effortlessly punch at him—as is the case with shadow boxing? From this simple example, we can learn that though shadow boxing may be an effective tool to help you loosen up and study the dynamic of your own punches, it is not an efficient training method to make you a more competent fighter.

SHADOW KICKING

The shadow-boxing style of home training is also commonly used among self-defense technicians who have mastered the basic elements of some of the various self-defense kicking applications. They generally, in an uncontrolled manner, powerfully drive their kicks into the air. Though this method of kick development is commonly taught in many martial arts schools, it is no doubt one of the most damaging things you can do to your knees, hips, and ankles.

By powerfully launching a kick into the open air, you snap your leg up and out, generally as high as your current level of stretching will allow your leg to go. By practicing your kicking technique in this fashion, you do not develop any degree of focus, and your leg joints can be easily damaged. For example, by propelling your leg forward and up in a Front Kick, you are forcefully snapping your knee. As time goes on, this type of powerful snapping to the knee will cause your cartilage and ligaments to unnaturally stretch and possibly tear. For some, this may take a long time to occur; for others, it may occur much more rapidly.

Very similar practices are used with various other kicks. The powerful air-driven Side Kick, for example, puts a great deal of pressure on the tendons in your hips. The powerful air-launched Roundhouse Kick can damage both your hip and knee joints. Therefore, these attempts at powerfully launching kicks into the air is not a good method of solitary home training.

EFFECTIVE HOME TRAINING

The two primary reasons for training in self-defense applications are physical fitness and the ability to successfully defend yourself if you ever encounter the need. Therefore, to remain well-versed in both, you must refine your home-training methods so you will not only gain superior technique and focusing ability, but maintain the health of your body, as well.

The question is obviously asked, "What type of effective home training can be practiced when I don't have a place to hang a heavy bag, and there is no training partner to hold a focus glove for me?" There are several safe and effective methods for the development of your fighting skills, which can be easily done in your home, even if you live in a small apartment.

OPEN AIR PUNCHING

To begin our understanding, let's first come to know what type of open air punching and kicking is safe and effective for focus development. As an open air punch is controlled by the very strong back and shoulder muscles, the ability to safely launch these random punches can be done with little worry of damaging your body, as long as you don't throw them with such power and lack of control that you allow your punching arm to overextend your shoulder or elbow joint.

It's important to keep in mind, especially in shadow-boxing home training, that no punch should be allowed to control the momentum of your body. Just as in the case of a punch directed toward a human target, you want to maintain control over all your movements and the elbow joint of your punching arm should always be allowed to remain slightly bent, even as your punch is being extended. With this, it will remain undamaged.

Prior to beginning home shadow-boxing training, you should loosen up your arms and shoulders. This is easily accomplished by rotating your shoulder in a circular fashion, back and forward, and then shaking your arms loose and moving them around a bit. From this, you will release any initial muscle tension and cause increased blood circulation to reach your arms and shoulders.

FOCUSED SHADOW BOXING

Once you have performed this initial warm-up, you can go into your open air punching. Ideally, you need to find a target to focus upon. This does not even have to be a target you will impact. It can be a location on your own body in a mirror, or a physical object some distance from you. In either case, this will give you an object to focus your attack upon, and by punching at an object instead of punching at the air, not only will your eye-to-hand focus improve, but you will be able to immediately notice if your punches would have made contact.

Very likely in the beginning of this shadow-boxing training, you will be amazed at how often the power of your arm will throw your punch off its intended target. As time goes on, and you continue this and your other self-defense training, you will come to understand how to effectively deliver your punches to compensate for your arm's muscle strength. You will eventually begin to make contact with your intended imaginary target.

During your punch oriented shadow boxing, you should constantly keep your body moving in boxer fashion, increasing your heart rate and training yourself to move like a fighter. In this way, you benefit both your cardiovascular system and your self-defense training. Again, you must remember, however, this imaginary training is limited in its effectiveness, and you should not believe it is actual impact-oriented target training.

FOCUSED SHADOW KICKING

Open air kicking is another common method of solo home training. Whenever you perform one of these open air kicks, especially at the early stages of your training, your kick should be executed slowly and driven precisely toward an imaginary opponent whom you have focused upon. With this style of open air kick-training you will substantially improve your various kicking techniques and your focus with your kicks will improve as well.

The reason most people want to powerfully kick at undefined objects is that the momentum gained by forcing their kick into the air with sheer muscular strength sends the kick higher than it will normally go. While the height of a kick may look impressive, the height has no bearing on the outcome of any actual physical confrontation.

If a kick is not properly delivered to your opponent, it will not be effective in a street encounter. For these reasons, whenever you perform an open air kick—be it a front-, side-, roundhouse-, or one of the more advanced kicks—by doing it slowly and repeating it numerous times, you will come to a clear understanding of the actual elements that make up the specific kick. You will understand which leg muscles are used in its application, and the proper body position to remain balanced when performing it. These are all things that no one can teach you. Though an instructor may attempt to explain them to you, it is only through conscious repeated practice that you will develop the deep understanding it takes to always perform each kick properly and precisely. This is what open air kick practice is designed to do.

Open air kicks should be performed slowly, and they should be focused on a physical target. As in the case of shadow boxing, you don't even need to make contact with the target. Through continued practice, you will find that you will have developed so much control through this type of focus training that you will be able to make very light contact with these physical objects and not damage them or your body.

TARGETS

The next step in solo home training to increase your focus and give you added timing is to suspend an object from your ceiling or doorway and use it as a strike target.

Many companies market various styles of striking targets designed to be suspended between your ceiling and the floor. When you strike at these types of targets, you instantly know if you have struck them in proper fashion. If you have, the target moves in a linear line: back and forth. If you have not, the target spins awkwardly out of control. This kind of solo training allows you to accurately develop focus and proper striking technique with both punching and kicking techniques.

If you don't want to buy one of these striking targets, an inexpensive alternative is to use an ordinary tennis or racket ball and tie a long string to it, and then hang it from your ceiling. This is also an ideal tool to help you in target focusing.

Reasons to Target

The refinement in your punching and kicking ability, which will be gained by targeting a small suspended object, is due to the fact that these targets are very defined in size and shape. Therefore, your offensive techniques must become very precise to make impact with them. Through continued training you can achieve a highly refined ability to strike exact locations. Thus, if you ever encounter an aggressive opponent in a street confrontation, you will possess the ability to effectively launch an exacting attack on him.

Placing Your Target

Whenever you position one of these striking balls or other targets for practice, you should always locate them in a position equivalent to a location you would actually strike on your opponent's body; for example—the head, solar plexus, groin, and so on. By locating these targets in approximate bodily strike locations, you will learn which offensive techniques are most effective and can be powerfully delivered to each region of your opponent's body.

PARTNER TRAINING

Partner training is, of course, the ideal way to develop your self-defense skills. By working with another individual you come to understand that human movement is predictable. Through ongoing practice, you can come to understand what movement follows the various types of punches or kicks, and how opponents react once their grasp has been dislodged, and so on. Thus, simply by practicing and evolving the various defensive techniques you have learned, you can become a more proficient self-defense technician.

Focus-Training with a Partner

In terms of focus-training for striking attacks: have your training partner hold two focus gloves that he keeps in constant motion. This is an ideal way to master striking focus. You will additionally come to master redeployment of your various punching and kicking techniques once your intended target has moved. In addition, you will come to understand how to instantly redeploy your offenses with a secondary attack if your first line of defense proves ineffective. To this end, simply have your training partner put on two highly available focus gloves and move, allowing you to punch, kick, and strike out. From this, you will quickly come to mastering effective striking techniques.

As you now have learned, to effectively progress in the realm of self-defense, you must give up the beautiful ritual of launching erratic (and inefficient) punches and kicks in the air. They look beautiful, but it is more realistic to practice conscious focus training at home, so that you may become a more efficient self-defense technician who possesses the ability to deliver powerful and precisely focused attacks on your opponent, if ever the need arises.

Conclusion

Being victorious in battle is easy.
Maintaining the victory is virtually impossible.
—WU TZU

I f you live your life at a confrontational level, you will constantly find battles. This type of lifestyle keeps you continually on edge, and just like a gunfighter of the Old West, there will always be somebody faster.

If you are a competent self-defense technician, you possess a clearly defined sense of self, and do not need to prove your validity via the conquest of others; you never seek out battle. If a confrontational situation finds you, deal with it in the most effective manner possible and then walk away, reentering a life of peace.

Ultimately, martial arts is not about fighting. It is about seeing. By consciously opening your eyes to the world around you, not only are you allowed to take in the beauty of your surroundings, but you see oncoming danger with a refined clarity not possessed by the average individual who passes through existence encased in a shell of predetermined emotions, desires, and fears. Seeing is your ultimate defense. For then you fight without fighting—you can leave before a confrontation ever begins.

Remember, the self-defense aspects of the martial arts, though founded thousands of years ago as a way of refined warfare, are no longer subject to those unenlightened definitions. Today, the martial arts can be your pathway to enlightenment. Through precise body and mind coordination, you refine your senses to the degree that each of your physical movements becomes an act of meditation.

Be like the river encountering a rock—flow with grace around any obstacle.

Suggested Reading

Aston, W. G., trans. *Nihongi*. Tokyo: Charles E. Tuttle, 1972.

Braveman, Arthur, trans. *Warrior of Zen: The Diamond-Hard Wisdom Mind of Suzuki Shosan*. Tokyo: Kodansha International, 1994.

The Dhammapada. Thomas Byrom, trans. New York: Vintage Books, 1976.

Cleary, Thomas, trans. *The Book of Leadership and Strategy: Lessons of the Chinese Masters: Translations from the Taoist Classic, Huainanzi*. Boston: Shambhala, 1992.

———. *The Japanese Art of War*. Boston: Shambhala, 1992.

Drager, Donn F. *Classical Bujutsu*. New York: Weatherhill, 1973.

———. *Classical Budo*. New York: Weatherhill, 1973.

———. *Modern Bujutsu and Budo*. New York: Weatherhill, 1974.

Friday, Karl F. and Seki Humitake. *Legacies of the Sword*. Honolulu: University of Hawaii Press, 1997.

Feng, Gia-Fu, trans. *Lao Tsu: Tao Te Ching*. New York: Vintage Books, 1971.

———. *Chuang Tsu: Inner Chapters*. New York: Vintage Books, 1974.

Giles, Lionel. *Sun Tzu on the Art of War*. Taipei: Taipei Master Press, 1972.

King, Winston, L. *Zen and the Way of the Samurai*. Oxford: Oxford University Press, 1993.

Liang, Zhuge and Liu Ji. *Mastering the Art of War*. Thomas Cleary, ed. Boston: Shambhala, 1986.

Major, John S., trans. *Heaven and Earth in Early Han Thought: Chapters Three, Four and Five of the Huainanzi*. Albany: SUNY Press, 1993.

Musashi, Miyamoto, *A Book of Five Rings*. Victor Harris, trans. Woodstock, NY: Overlook Press, 1974.

Ratti, Oscar and Adele Westbrook. *Secrets of the Samurai*. Tokyo: Charles E. Tuttle, 1973.

Sato, Hiroaki, *Legends of the Samurai*. Woodstock, NY: Overlook Press, 1995.

———. *The Mind and the Sword*. Woodstock, NY: Overlook Press, 1986.

Sawyer, Ralph D., trans. *Sun-Tzu: The Art of War*. New York: Barnes and Noble, 1994.

———, trans. *The Art of the Warrior*. Boston: Shambhala, 1996.

———, trans. *The Seven Military Classics of Ancient China*. Boulder: Westview Press, 1993.

Schwartz, Benjamin I. *The World of Thought in Ancient China*. Cambridge: Harvard University Press, 1985.

Storry, Richard. *The Way of the Samurai*. New York: Galley Press, 1978.

Sun, Pin and Pin-Ping Sun, *The Art of the Warrior: Leadership and Strategy from the Chinese Military Classics*. Ralph D. Sawyer, trans., Mei-chun Sawyer, ed. Boston: Shambhala, 1996.

Tsunetomo, Yamamoto. *Hagakura*. William Scott Wilson, trans. Tokyo: Kondansha International, 1979.

Turnbull, S. R. *The Samurai: A Military History*. New York: Macmillan, 1977.

Tzu, Sun, and Pin Tzu. *The Complete Art of War*. Boulder: Westview Press, 1996.

Select Bibliography

Aston, W. G., trans. *Nihongi*. Tokyo: Charles E. Tuttle, 1972.

The Dhammapada. Thomas Byrom, trans. New York: Vintage Books, 1976.

Feng, Gia-Fu, trans. *Lao Tsu: Tao Te Ching*. New York: Vintage Books, 1971.

———, trans. *Chuang Tsu: Inner Chapters*. New York: Vintage Books, 1974.

Drager, Donn F. *Classical Bujutsu*. New York: Weatherhill, 1973.

———. *Classical Budo*. New York: Weatherhill, 1973.

———. *Modern Bujutsu and Budo*. New York: Weatherhill, 1974.

King, Winston L. *Zen and the Way of the Samurai*. Oxford: Oxford University Press, 1993.

Legge, James. *The Four Books*. Hong Kong: Private Publication, 1861.

Musashi, Miyamoto *A Book of Five Rings*. Victor Harris, trans. Woodstock, NY: Overlook Press, 1974.

Ratti, Oscar and Adele Westbrook. *Secrets of the Samurai*. Tokyo: Charles E. Tuttle, 1973.

Sato, Hiroaki. *Legends of the Samurai*. Woodstock, NY: Overlook Press, 1995.

———. *The Mind and the Sword*. Woodstock, NY: Overlook Press, 1986.

Sawyer, Ralph D., trans. *Sun-Tzu: The Art of War*. New York: Barnes and Noble, 1994.

————, trans. *The Art of the Warrior*. Boston: Shambhala, 1996.

Storry, Richard. *The Way of the Samurai*. New York: Galley Press, 1978.

Tsunetomo, Yamamoto. *Hagakura*. William Scott Wilson, trans. Tokyo: Kondansha International, 1979.

Turnbull, S. R. *The Samurai: A Military History*. New York: Macmillan, 1977.

Index

Scott Shaw is one of the preeminent Martial Arts Masters of the Western world. He began his study of the martial arts as a young boy. Today he is one of the world's most advanced Masters of the Korean martial art of Hapkido. In addition, he holds Master Certification in Taekwondo and Aikijutsu. Shaw is at the forefront of integrating spirituality into the modern martial arts. During his youth he became deeply involved in Eastern mysticism. He studied meditation with some of the great teachers of our time and has been formally initiated into Yogic and Buddhist sects. For over two decades Scott has returned to Asia to document obscure aspects of Asian culture in words and on film, and to refine his martial and meditative understanding.

Scott Shaw lives in southern California and is the author of *Simple Bliss* (Element Books), *Samurai Zen* (Weiser), *Zen O'clock* (Weiser), *The Ki Process: Korean Secrets for Cultivating Dynamic Energy* (Weiser), *The Warrior is Silent: Martial Arts and the Spiritual Path* (Inner Traditions), and *Hapkido: The Korean Art of Self-Defense* (Tuttle).